THE VARIABLE LIFE

The Variable Life

Finding Clarity and Confidence
in a World of Choices

John Weirick

 BRDDG

"Mixing memoir with spiritual insights, *The Variable Life* challenges readers to know their own stories, re-examine the turning points in their lives and see what God has been teaching them through all the victories and the hardships. John Weirick encourages readers to ask big questions, take risks and move forward with confidence. If you feel stuck, scared or insecure, this book is for you."

— *Dargan Thompson, writer, editor, and former editor at RELEVANT Magazine*

"John Weirick looks at life through the lens of an introvert who's determined to leave the comfortable and embrace everything life has to offer. Refreshingly honest and inspiring, a must read for Millennials!"

— *Beth Marshall, author of Grief Survivor: 28 Steps Toward Hope and Healing*

"When I read *The Variable Life*, I kept thinking to myself, 'Thank you, God, for someone who takes the time to think through and write about the stuff of life I should probably process.' Few people live with more intentionality and take such radical inventory of their life as John. *The Variable Life* is a gift for us all: We'll find ourselves stirred as we, too, remember those big moments in life when we asked, 'God, you got me here?' And we'll find ourselves moved from our comfy couches and into the lives of the people around us."

— *Nate Ray, pastor and speaker*

"Everyone wants the benefit of change, but few people engage the process of change; John is one of those few people. The beauty of this project, though, is that it's not some sort of self-righteous or self-promoting work, but rather an invitation to search the variables in your own life and to navigate the experiences that have shaped your story thus far and those which will shape the parts of your story yet to be experienced. You'll be encouraged, challenged, inspired, and best of all, supported by someone who's walking the journey with you."

— *Ricky and Krista Ortiz, pastor and speaker, writer*

"Weaving truths through his unique style of storytelling, John calls readers into a deeper connection with the author and creator of our stories. Reading *The Variable Life* helped me see how I can grow healthy relationships without losing myself in the process."

— *Stephanie Long, writer and editor at Redeemed For More*

Available from Amazon.com and other retail outlets.

Library of Congress Control Number: 2017901602
CreateSpace Independent Publishing Platform, North Charleston, SC

ISBN-13: 978-1542857208

ISBN-10: 1542857201

Printed in the United States of America

Book cover and interior design by Ben Coleman for www.brddg.is
Author photo by Evan Oliver for www.theolivers.co
Edited by Chantel Hamilton for www.afterwordscommunications.com

To Kati
for walking with me through all the variables

Contents

Author's Note   1

1 Prologue   3

MOVEMENT ONE: FORMATION

2 Prayers of a Super Bowl Champion   9
3 The Variable Life   15
4 Getting the Call   19
5 On the Verge   21
6 Faded Red Plastic Sled   25
7 Making Friends   31
8 The Edge of the Cornfield   35
9 Curing Loneliness   39
10 Dressed Up   45
11 Little Things are the Big Things   51
12 Sunday School Liar   55
13 Saved from Mediocrity   59

MOVEMENT TWO: DISRUPTION

14 Seeing the Invisible   67
15 The Electrical Soil   71
16 Middle School Romance   77
17 Meeting the Girl   83
18 In the Wilderness   89
19 Getting Out of Safe Mode   95
20 The Lost Get Found   101
21 Private School   105
22 The Marks of a Servant   111
23 What God Wants   117

24 Down on the Farm   123
25 Significant Work   127
26 Group Showers   131

MOVEMENT THREE: REFINEMENT

27 When Love Isn't Sexy   137
28 Brotherhood   145
29 Not Easily Surrendered   149
30 Game Boys and the Abundant Life   155
31 When God Speaks   159
32 What We Can't Have   165
33 Basketball   169
34 God on the Whiteboard   175
35 How to Be Refreshed   179
36 A Package from the Past   185
37 Running from the Nourishment We Need   189

MOVEMENT FOUR: INTEGRATION

38 The Fleeting Moment   197
39 The Pressures of Marriage   201
40 Facing Our Flaws   207
41 Seeing Through Screens   213
42 Instagram and the Power of Yes   219
43 Sleeping Through the American Dream   227
44 Hoping for Home   233
45 A Taste of Heaven   239
46 Adventures Worth Sharing   247
47 An Evening with the Elderly   253
48 Don't Give Up   257
49 The End of the Road   261

50 Epilogue   267
    Notes   271
    Thanks   277
    About the Author   283

Author's Note

If you and I sat down for coffee, I would ask you about the most important moments of your life. And as you shared your stories, you would realize none of those moments would have happened unless you made a choice and something changed.

Your life is the story of the choices you make.

Philosopher René Descartes said, "If you would be a real seeker after truth, it is necessary that at least once in your life you doubt, as far as possible, all things."[1]

I wrote this book to discover the truth about who I am becoming and to help you discover the truth about yourself, too.

Finding the truth about ourselves and the world requires risk, a willingness to challenge our assumptions and admit we need to change. I was a timid, compliant introvert who would rather stay home than taste adventure or make new friends. I believed what I was told about God and how to live until I began to search on my own terms. Yet the more questions I asked, the less satisfying neat and tidy answers became.

This is what I know: life is a maze of choices, and God is somewhere to be found. Discovering the truth about ourselves lies at that intersection. It's amazing what you'll find when you walk through this world with your heart and mind open, willing to embrace life's variables.

The goal of this book is not to convince you to believe everything I believe. Consider this a collection of working theories for which I haven't found all the answers. You have permission to disagree; I'll probably change my mind, too, before the year is out, but I hope to befriend you with these words on this part of our journey together.

You might face the variables of a new job, the end of a relationship you thought would last much longer, or the start of a new decade with a clean slate. Perhaps you're choosing which college to attend, when to start a family, or how to juggle all the commitments you've already made. Every choice you make is another step through the maze of variables.

Wherever you are, whatever you do, thank you for joining me in these pages. I hope they help you find clarity and confidence in your own world of choices.

John

1

Prologue

"You may not know it yet, but you're going to write a book some day."

It caught me by surprise. I stood frozen for a moment, listening to that sentence hang in the air.

The night was getting late, so I kneeled to tie my shoes. Conversations with my friend and his father, Bob, dragged well into the evening. Their family frequently welcomed me into their home, but this was the first time Bob told me something like that, about a book. My life wasn't worthy of any words.

Status Quo

My friend and I were seniors in high school. He's one of the most personable people I know—the kind of person who's never met a stranger, shakes your hand politely, and wears an eager grin like he's sincerely glad to meet you. His tall, lanky frame and neatly combed brown hair reminds you of the kid who always played sports at recess and went to band camp mostly to make friends—which is exactly what he did. And when he parted ways, it was always with a hug from his long arms, like you'd known him for years and you'd just had a good conversation.

We stayed up late most nights at my house or his, dreaming about the freedoms of pending college life. Late-night television tropes and Conan O'Brien's squirrelly humor weaseled their way into our personalities. We had convinced our parents to forgo curfews, since we were enrolled as high school students at the local community college. The late-morning classroom hours afforded us precious time to sleep in, while our high school peers had to get up early. We passed the time by sitting on the couch and wishing for exciting lives.

I thought exciting lives belonged only to people who mattered, who were popular for achieving something great or being picture-perfect humans. I knew enough about my own life to know I hadn't been through anything worth writing or reading about. I hadn't overcome great obstacles to make a name for myself or changed the world, and, probably like you, I didn't think stories from my life were worth sharing.

It was during that year that I rediscovered the value of books, having largely neglected leisurely reading since completing *The Lord of the Rings* a couple years prior. My appetite was changing, trading in fiction titles for practical living and trying to understand God. I didn't want to be entertained by literature as much as I wanted to learn from it and grow.

Heroic figures amazed me—the ones who endured when everything around them changed, who faced their fears and the conflicts that threatened to silence their lives. I grew jealous of the camaraderie that all great characters found on their journeys, connecting deeply with the very people who could help them move forward.

Sitting on the cusp of adulthood made me realize there was a lot I didn't understand. Simplistic, childish ways of thinking disguised themselves as adolescent machismo, flaws I thought had disappeared in my mental rearview mirror. I was an introvert who knew I needed people, but I despised it as a weakness because I didn't feel connected or liked in most social situations. My own lack of self-awareness kept me from seeing how blind I really was, yet I felt some sort of magnetic pull beyond the norm. If people in great stories grew through change, conflict, and relationships, I had to adapt, too. I wanted to read non-fiction. I wanted to live it even more. That night, things began to change. In the midst of life transitions that would propel me to grow and change, I gathered that there was a story for which I was destined to fill in the details. The expectations of a typical life of routine and rigidity seemed too small a space to be boxed in. If it were true that "every good thing that has happened in your life happened because something changed," accepting the status quo was unacceptable.[2] I couldn't explain it at that time, in the developing parts of my story, but I sensed the need to experience more, to do more, and to be more.

One Small Remark

When I told Bob about a few of the books I planned to read, as I stood by the door, he paused for a moment. He was one of the wise mentor figures in my life—bespectacled, kind, and thoughtful—sort of an adopted uncle because of my close friendship with his sons. I respected Bob and tried to listen to whatever he said, because he knew a lot about God and life and had loads of books lining his home office walls.

"I think you'll do it; you'll write a book."

I brushed off the remark with polite nonchalance. Bob was a smart guy, but I didn't think I'd ever do any such thing.

I didn't lead a noteworthy, variable life; I lived a stagnant one. And with such an unremarkable life, I didn't think I had anything to say.

MOVEMENT ONE

Formation

2

Prayers of a Super Bowl Champion

"The art of living lies less in eliminating
our troubles than in growing with them."

BERNARD M. BARUCH

Spring in Minnesota is something of an enigma. At times, the sun shines and beckons one outdoors, only to find the bitter cold air hasn't left with the winter white. A snowstorm or two usually dumps another blanket of heavy powder on the sandy, salty roads. When the sun comes out again and the temperature flirts with the freezing point, a brown slush covers roadways until the green of true spring begins to show on budding trees and dormant lawns.

As was typical of the past four months, I sauntered into work, doing my best to ignore the cold March wind. I didn't want to be in Rochester, my hometown, embittered by winter and feeling stuck when my life was supposed to be taking off. Even God was bored with my life; I wasn't even sure he cared, or if he did, why he wasn't doing something about it.

I was grateful my parents allowed me to move back into their house after I graduated from college, but I wanted to be somewhere else, anywhere else. My hopes of landing a career-sized job right after graduation quickly faded as I heard phrases like "current recession" and "worst since the Great Depression" in the same sentence, though I did manage to get hired by an electronics store after a couple interviews.

This wasn't the first time I had interviewed at the store. During high school, I submitted my best handwritten application, repeatedly called managers, and arrived for a first interview in a poorly fastened necktie and disheveled hair. The blond manager was chipper and deliberate, as her pantsuit suggested, but she had no interest in conversation after she viewed my scarce, unimpressive résumé. I did not get the job.

The same manager interviewed me when I applied the second time, after college. My lack of confidence was still hanging around, but it was hidden a little better. She didn't seem to remember me. When she saw on my résumé that I had interned at a Top 40 morning show for a Minneapolis radio station, she eagerly told me how long she'd listened to that show and which funny bits and phone pranks were her favorites. I mustered up some chuckles and recalled a few specific stories of antics at the radio station. She ate it up. I got the job.

Months went by. I worked at the store while continuing the search of a career-launching radio job. Like countless other Millennials, I had a bachelor's degree, but I could get nothing more than this entry-level position. Surely, months of halfheartedly assisting customers had to end soon with a perfect offer from a radio station in a big city where I already had friends, like Atlanta, Nashville, or Chicago. That's what I thought I wanted.

Business as Unusual

That first day of March began as any other in the months I'd been working there. Mid-morning, a clean-cut, athletic-looking man in his late twenties approached the camera section with a brown-haired, attractive woman a few years younger. I wanted to avoid them, to be honest. My cynical nature often passed judgment on people before they even knew court was in session. But I knew I had a job to do, and I couldn't hide away from opportunities just because they required courage and hard work.

They seemed bearable. I tried to bide time by walking back to my register, attempting to look busy but really just wanting to go home and give up on my job.

Something in me wouldn't let me zone out.

I reluctantly made my way over to the display, where they were handling a few cameras in comparison. The man intended to surprise his wife with a camera package for her birthday, so he and his sister had arrived eager to make a purchase.

I walked them through the pros and cons of a few models, while prodding for a few more details. The man mentioned photo editing software on his Apple computer.

"What other software do you run on your Mac?" I asked.

The man answered, "Oh, I record music with Pro Tools and a few other things."

Pro Tools was one of the audio production programs I'd used in college, an industry standard. I pressed him for more.

"So, you write music? What do you play?"

"Yeah, I play guitar and sing. Usually Taylor guitars and some piano."

"Do you have anything posted online?"

He introduced himself as Ben and mentioned his website. "I'll have to look that up after work. What kind of music is it?"

He didn't look like a pop musician. His build was more like that of an athlete or a nightclub bouncer.

He explained that he released music on a label based in Nashville, and performed on small tours.

I told them about my love for music—both listening and playing— and travel, too. Ben mentioned something about a return trip to Cincinnati.

Closing the sale, I paused and turned to Ben. "What do you do in Cincinnati?"

"I play football."

I'm sure my mouth dropped a little. "The Cincinnati Bengals? As in the NFL?"

Ben smiled humbly and said he'd even won a Super Bowl ring with a different team a couple years before.

"So I'm selling a camera to a Super Bowl champion?"

He shrugged it off, but seemed to appreciate the recognition. After finishing the purchase, Ben and his sister stopped me before I could walk away.

"Hey John, how can we pray for you today?"

My mind froze. Work wasn't a place I talked about religion or God. It required too much effort and risked coworkers' scorn. I thought about the kind of person I was supposed to be and wondered if that was the kind of person I wanted to be. But then I started talking.

"Um...Honestly, I need a new job."

Their eyebrows raised in silent curiosity.

I told them about my growing impatience during the months of job searching: how I'd been hoping for a new, clear path of career opportunities that never came. It felt like a mini therapy session, but only my complaints voiced without solutions given. Ben and his sister stepped closer to me and said a brief prayer, asking God to do something more with my work, my ambitions, and my life.

The moment grew surreal in a heightened awareness, but when Ben said "amen," I couldn't find anything to say except "thanks."

And like any other ordinary customers, they walked out the front door into the blustery March day.

Unprepared

Earlier that morning, before work, I'd read something especially poignant for the day I was about to live. A long time ago, a man named Paul wrote to people who were having trouble figuring things out and weren't where they needed to be. Before he closed the letter, he wrote: "Be on your guard; stand firm in the faith; be courageous; be strong. Do everything in love."[3]

It's hard to know when to be attentive for the best moments in life. They seem to show up unexpectedly. If we're not careful, these times will slip by unnoticed, like a leaf swept down the current of a river. And over time, faith slowly erodes. When the object of our hopes is still far on the horizon and we don't seem to be making progress toward it, faith is the first casualty.

To tell you the truth, there were many days of frustration and helplessness as I worked that job. I instinctively knew that "life is a process of becoming, a combination of states we have to go through. Where people fail is that they wish to elect a state and remain in it. This is a kind of death."[4] I didn't want to live the slow death of monotony. Sure, I could've quit and gotten something else lined up, but I was waiting on something else to unfold. I was hoping in something I wasn't even sure would happen. I expected an entry-level radio position would be offered a month into job searching, not eight.

I wasn't being strong like that writer Paul talked about. I felt weak and out of control of my own existence. I certainly wasn't being courageous or doing everything with an attitude of love. Love is risky, and I was risk averse.

In the midst of our routine, staying faithful in the daily grind of our work, our play, and our living, God meets us in a way we did not expect. He always brings changes. The changes are rarely what we expect, but they are ultimately for our good because he is.

Perhaps that's the state God likes to find us in: vulnerable but expectant. Waiting for a new transition only works when we prepare to take the next step.

I couldn't have guessed the next step in my story, not in a hundred years.

3

The Variable Life

Every life is a story.

Life plays like a movie, but it doesn't quite pan out. The scenes often feel contrived or insignificant—disjointed, awkward, and boring all at the same time. Maybe a life with clear direction is too elusive for most of us to grasp.

I can see myself in third person, as a character enveloped in a story, and so are you: in a neighborhood, in a city, in a nation and a world. Hundreds and thousands and millions of people filling up the empty space between tall buildings, on roads, and in fields and forests, but few of the people are connected to each other or to me.

There must be a bigger story going on, something that ties us all together and spans bridges and miles, through cities and forests. Perhaps it's an invisible network received only by those of us who listen with keen awareness for most of our lives, yearning for something more.

If God is real, the big story must involve him, too. I've heard it said that God is an author, writing out the screenplay of our lives and handing the script down to us to see if we'll say yes and play a part. Some days it feels like the script we've been assigned is too difficult; the words don't seem right coming out of our mouths. Other days the script seems to fit perfectly, as we find we've done just what we were supposed to at that moment—the reward of doing what is right and good and fitting. As a character in a story, I sense I must do something, be somebody, but I do not know what. I am stuck in a state of confusion, an internal wrestling match between the will, the heart, and the mind. Each of us is a protagonist in our own way, yet a fragment of truth buried in our chests tells us there is a bigger story than our own. Each of our stories is made to match up with the next, like a puzzle spread across the kitchen table, interconnected fearfully and wonderfully.

We see signs of longing for a culmination of the big story. Resolution tugs at our hearts, though we've been stuck in the middle of the same settings and same dialogue for so many chapters, but change is calling. Change is always calling.

The variables present in a lifetime of decisions can be staggering: so many places to go, people to meet, and things to see. The sheer volume of available opportunities can paralyze us before we can even get into the real plot of our life stories.

The world is wide, and the horizon still far off. A 21st century interconnected globe means many of us have the opportunity to do nearly anything we want to, limited only by the scope of our pursuits. It's true; some things require money or status or access, but the underlying factors shaping our stories are the choices we make in a world of endless possibilities.

"Grace / to be born and live as variously as possible."[5] There's a lot of grace injected into our stories from the onset. God, in his wisdom and kindness, hands us a pen. We're offered a chance to co-write a story with the author of all life. There may be times when I'll defer to his plot, or times when he'll let me wander around in a few deviating subplots, but he always beckons me back to writing the story with him. The story is better when we write together.

When we write together, life makes more sense and offers richer rewards. I am compelled to grow the most when I face inescapable change, when I endure inevitable conflict, when I embrace the transforming power of relationships. I find clarity and confidence in a world of choices.

When God and I conspire on the next chapters of my life, he tells me not to be afraid, that he will walk with me through the tangled web of possibilities. And he tells me the only way forward is through these changes, conflicts, and relationships. If we are to become the people we're meant to be, we must embrace these variables. It is the way of humanity's story.

Still, we hold these variables loosely, with open hands, because nothing is guaranteed: "You must wake up every morning knowing that no promise is unbreakable, least of all the promise of waking up at all."[6]

You've got to forge a path out of all the choices before you. If you've got to be somebody in this story, to accomplish something meaningful, you'll have to make sense of all the different options, embracing some and rejecting the rest. You can make this story count for something. This is the struggle for significance. This is the human condition. This is your variable life.

4

Getting the Call

"Your career makes a living but your calling makes your life."
RICK WARREN

That March afternoon, after a Super Bowl champion prayed for me and my dead-end career, I received a phone call from a 541 area code. I didn't know what part of the country had a 541 area code. I answered the phone to be greeted by a radio company I had sent a résumé to a few months earlier. The company invited me to submit a formal application for the job.

I was eager for a chance to enter the broadcasting industry, but still a bit skeptical after the few rejections and the many dozens of ignored calls and hundreds of e-mails to other companies. I began to understand why people talked about the terrible recession so much: "Tell me about despair, yours, and I will tell you mine."[7] It seemed like a losing battle, and I was running out of rations of hope for my own work future. Rejections became more emotional and morphed into near desperation.

Nonetheless, I sent in the formal application to the radio company with the 541 area code and waited. A week later, they scheduled a phone interview and asked about my work experience. I told them about my years as a college radio DJ, programming music, planning show segments, producing ads, recording voiceovers, and other things radio producers do.

They asked what I would do if I were running an audio control board and something went awry. Real radio producers know what to do in a pinch. I told them I would play backup music and restart the computers or something like that. I made it up as I talked, and pretended to be a grownup.

During the phone interview, I asked a bit about the company, what the people are like, and about the Oregonian city in which the company was located. Somehow, I got a second phone interview two weeks later and was welcomed to the team. My dream was happening. I was becoming a real radio producer.

Six weeks after getting the first call from a 541 number, my bags were packed and the car was stuffed with belongings. I set foot on Oregon soil. My career as a professional broadcaster had begun—a new chapter in a story I had never expected.

5

On the Verge

*"The purpose of life is to live it, to taste experience
to the utmost, to reach out eagerly and without fear
for newer and richer experience."*

ELEANOR ROOSEVELT

It was April, a month after the Super Bowl champion prayed
for me. I packed the bare essentials of my belongings and headed west. My parents flew out to help me settle into my new city.

My job producing radio programs in Southern Oregon was
the kind of job you'd think would be only in major metropolitan
centers like New York or Los Angeles. As a place I'd never been
to, it seemed large and distinct. I felt too small, too inconsequential to be there and work a real adult job. I almost talked
myself out of it before I even started.

We arrived on a Saturday, stepping off the plane to the sight
of mountains in every direction. I stood on the tarmac for a moment to take it in. Minnesota didn't have mountains. Oregon
had endless rolling green ones with multiple distant peaks.

That night in our hotel room, while my parents snored out
their jet lag on the next bed over, I lay quietly reflecting on the
change life had propelled me into. I was on the verge of something utterly new, and I felt the pressure. It was all real, the
wonderful and terrible opportunity to test the limits of my resolve in a new adventure away from everything I'd ever known.

I couldn't sleep. I didn't know what else to do, so I read a few Psalms and typed out thoughts that would become the first post on my blog since I had traveled during college several years before.

Blog Post: Digital Scribbles from a Hotel Room

How did I get here? How did this happen? Be careful, my friends, for when you ask, you may receive. When you inquire the direction of a God who listens to his children, he may just reply with a "yes." He answered my request for a radio position to launch a career with. But he opened this door 2,000 miles from the place I've called home for all the years of my life.

Not having even seen the city, it represents something of a completely cold jump into foreign surroundings. This civilization nestled in a river valley of possibility, carved into the western Cascade Range, is now the place I'll call home for the next chapter of my life.

My friends: "Come and see what God has done, his awesome deeds for mankind!"[8]

I have no doubt in my mind that this is from him, and it is a gift that I must pursue. And when my ability fails, when I've lost patience for adjusting to new grocery stores and having gas attendants and learning a new job in an unfamiliar state, it is then that he says, "I am here for you. I am with you and feel these emotions and tiredness with you. I won't take away these difficulties, but I will walk with you through them. I'm with you for the long haul. Trust me."

"We went through fire and water, but you brought us to a place of abundance."[9]

And in this vein God says, "I know this is hard. This is not comfortable. This is not easy, but it is right, and it is the best possible thing for your benefit down the road. You will have all you need in me because I will take care of you."

God's provided this radio job, this opportunity to relocate to a beautiful state, and I trust he will provide housing, roommates, solid friends, a good church, and meaningful relationships with coworkers.

"You crown the year with your bounty, and your carts overflow with abundance."[10]

It is not without sadness that I leave friends and family behind. I am relocating away from some of the closest friends a person could ask for. I anticipate the times I can visit them, and they me, for those times will be all the sweeter. But it is because I believe this is worth it.

In years to come, I imagine I will look back at this time with a grateful heart because it was such a profound transition in my life that God has used to remind me, "I'm with you; I'm for you."

"Come and hear, all you who fear God; let me tell you what he has done for me."[11]

New Roots

Those next few days and weeks were filled with constant questions running through my mind, wondering if God would really provide what I thought—and desperately hoped—he would.

Some of the emotions that evolved from my inner monologue were unexpected and uninvited. Yet new adventures and new perspectives are refreshing like the spring rains in the Northwest, pushing up green life from the brown forest floors, begging my spirit to do the same. If we must take adventures in order to know where we truly belong, I took a leap in the right direction, but so many variables remained.

Relearning how to make friends wasn't as fun after a while. I just wanted people to know me, to be there for me and understand what I was going through. But the depth of rich friendships can't be grown quickly, especially not for introverts. Roots need time to get beyond the shallow layers.

Perhaps it's true that nothing of lasting value comes easy. If that's the case, you and I have a good deal of work and dedication ahead of us. It's like God hands us the reins, smiles, and says, *Alright, now it's your turn. Give it a shot.*

6

Faded Red Plastic Sled

"I hope you live a life you're proud of. And if not,
I hope you have the strength to start all over again."

F. SCOTT FITZGERALD

The sky loomed dreary and gray, but spirits were high. Just like each day of a bleak Minnesota midwinter, children bound in wool and down coats, and topped with oversized stocking hats, emerged throughout the neighborhood. Every year, I was one of them: little, brightly colored blimps floating about the frozen yards, weaving through barren trees. It was practically a scene out of *A Charlie Brown Christmas*. I even checked the mail sometimes.

The daily ventures orbited around several activities, not unlike the Winter Olympics, except we had no torch. (My mother didn't want her children to play with fire.) Once the driveway was shoveled clear of fresh snow, the piles on the boulevard were tall and sturdy enough to dig cave fortresses in, which also served as snowball ammunition reserves. Making snow angels in the powder was a competition, producing undeniable evidence of sibling rivalry with my younger brother, Lee. He was shorter than me and had a smaller frame, but he easily had more muscle, which made him a worthy adversary in our winter games.

Another contest required serious leg power and cardio-vascular endurance by taking turns pulling the other in the faded red plastic sled—over lawns, up hills, through the faithful pines. It's amazing the kind of energy we had as eight- or ten-year-olds, especially trudging endlessly through the powder. And then there was the main event: downhill sledding.

One afternoon, I struck out in the suburban tundra alone, faded red plastic sled in tow. Filling the void of a human audience, the trees stood tall in anticipation. After conquering the front lawn's modest grade, I approached the crest of a hill I'd often overlooked: the abrupt slope between my parents' house and the neighbors'.

My pre-takeoff preparations were like poetry, every motion purposeful: positioning the faded red plastic sled on the precipice of the slope, packing my small frame into the vehicle of glory, and pulling the tow rope tight over my heavy boots to avoid dragging with extra friction.

Then it was time for the launch.

The exhilaration.

The cold wind on my face.

The shattering glass.

I did not expect the shattering glass, nor the deafening silence that followed.

It felt like emerging from the rubble of a bombed building, or the crushed furniture from a bar fight.

Dazed with disbelief, I checked for my legs: still intact.

The sled: virtually unharmed.

My weighty winter boots: hanging through a split-level living room window.

My ego: splintered more than the jagged glass.

Fallout

I sat dejected, the only smudge of ugly in the picturesque winter world. The climb back up the hill was more taxing than other days. I preferred not to tell my parents, but I knew I had no choice. Multiplying fear would envelop my young mind if I tried to keep it secret.

My father didn't seem angry when I told him I crashed through the neighbors' living room window. His eyes sat inquisitive and patient behind his thick glasses as I explained. I was surprised, hopeful, and terrified all at the same time. Something about it just felt guilty. Then my father walked with me to the neighbors' front door and made me tell a short, kind woman that I broke something of hers. She wasn't angry, either, just sort of quietly sad about it, but she didn't want me to feel bad. As we walked back home, my father told me to gather my allowance money.

Regrets

That kind of deflation feels like enslavement to failure. Consequences follow and shortfalls must be addressed; sometimes those regrets chain us down. Barriers keep us from moving forward. Guilt paralyzes us.

We all have regrets about our past. The worst ones are the ones we won't admit. It's easier to beat ourselves up over things we can't change than to accept the messy mistakes of our former selves. The difference is in the direction we face and the direction we move. Rather than wallow in regret, we are offered second, third, and thousandth chances. We are offered new beginnings, a fresh start.

We are offered grace.

It reminds me of Lamentations, a short book in the Bible that is really a downer except for one part in the middle. It's as if the brooding author paused for a moment, picked up his head, and looked toward the heavens, realizing the world isn't always doom and gloom. There are lots of imperfections in people and relationships and systems, but there is also good:

The thought of my suffering and homelessness is

bitter beyond words. I will never forget this awful time, as I grieve over my loss. Yet I still dare to hope when I remember this:

...The Lord is good to those who depend on him, to those who search for him. So it is good to wait quietly for salvation from the Lord. And it is good for people to submit at an early age to the yoke of his discipline.

Let them sit alone in silence beneath the Lord's demands. Let them lie face down in the dust, for there may be hope at last. Let them turn the other cheek to those who strike them and accept the insults of their enemies.

For no one is abandoned by the Lord forever. Though he brings grief, he also shows compassion because of the greatness of his unfailing love.

For he does not enjoy hurting people or causing them sorrow.[12]

Sometimes we're so wrapped up in the failures we've committed that we forget God's been nearby all along. It's not that he doesn't see our mistakes or we have to hide from him. The miraculous thing about God is he accepts us as we are, failures and all, then helps us change to get past the mistakes that hold us down.

When we encounter grace in light of our failures, we experience part of a better way of life Jesus talked about.[13] We are saved from a guilt-ridden conscience and from our failure. There are still consequences we will face, yet he has not abandoned us; he is for us.

That grace is what we need in our relationships, inadequate plans, and every choice we will ever make. Grace teaches us to be unafraid in the myriad of life's complexities. It equips us to stumble forward—learning to walk in faith, trusting the God who forgives.

Author Anne Lamott's words resonate: "I do not at all understand the mystery of grace—only that it meets us where we are but does not leave us where it found us."[14]

That was the grace I needed in new surroundings, when I felt alone in Oregon and when I knew I should start friendships but feared I wouldn't be able to, afraid I had made a huge mistake. It was what I needed on the days I missed my family and friends in Minnesota and wanted to give up and go back. Grace reminds us we have all we need.

No more hiding. No more guilt. No more fear.

The next winter of my childhood, I dug the faded red plastic sled out of the attic and stepped out into the white.

7

Making Friends

*"A journey is best measured in friends
rather than miles."*

TIM CAHILL

I first met Brian when I was six or seven. We attended the same church in Southeast Minnesota. His family moved to the East Coast when I was in second grade, but I was glad to see them return a few years later. In middle school and early high school, Brian and I spent more time together, talking about the latest albums from our favorite bands and going on mission trips and to youth camps around the Midwest.

Brian is the kind of friend you can't help but be grateful for: easygoing, dependable, and always finding a cool website or useful tech gadget before anyone else you know. I don't remember the moment I met him, but that's how steadfast he is. Brown eyes under short dark brown hair, ever hunting for practical knowledge, and always tinkering with something on a computer or a car.

Giving people the benefit of the doubt is something I've never been good at, but it seems to come naturally for him. Brian's calm smile makes you believe you can trust him; then he quotes a funny movie and you laugh together.

The Brothers

My sophomore year, a family moved to Rochester from rural Iowa. Brian and I met two tall, thin, long-armed brothers at a birthday party hosted by some families we knew at another church in town. Seth was outgoing with a goofy smile that revealed braces, and he wore a polo shirt tucked into his jeans and the cleanest white tennis shoes I had ever seen. Nate, the older brother, was friendly but a little more reserved—straight, dark brown hair styled like he was in a punk band, and clothes to match. They seemed like decent guys, but I was an introvert who wasn't one for talking to new people.

That fall, Seth and Nate attended an all-night event my church hosted at a local athletic club. Brian and I grew tired from playing basketball and swimming with people we knew, so our interests turned to the acoustic guitar and djembe the tall Iowans brought. We walked over to say hello and listened to them play a few songs, and we decided to hang out with them throughout the night. They weren't too bad for being from Iowa.

Over that year, the four of us shared more late nights, jam sessions, and involved conversations. Something I began to notice about this group of guys was their passion for doing things that mattered, particularly in relation to their faith. Those conversations weren't just typical teenage laments of first-world problems or shallowly glazing small-talk topics. They actually thought deeply about ideas, or at least tried to. They asked questions that challenged the status quo and sought perspective on how things should be instead of criticizing, blaming, and demeaning people who thought otherwise.

That was different than my rigid, restrictive paradigm. Our differences were building the foundation of a lesson I wouldn't learn outright until much later: "You are the product of the voices in your life. And it's up to you to decide who to listen to."[15]

What Good Friends Do

My new friends made me wonder if there was a more mature, passionate, and assertive version of myself buried somewhere in my chest, the kind of person I sensed I should be.

Good friends draw you out of your comfortable, routine self to enter into greater possibility for who you might become.

Challenging each other leads to growing with each other. A refined, renewed identity emerges from the variables of a connected life.

The best way to grow as an individual is to take on the challenges of life with a friend by your side, with a community that has your back no matter what. Even social science tells us close relationships do more for our health and happiness than medication or technological advances.[16] In real friendships, we're moved to risk more, dream more, and become more than we are. There is more to life than we're experiencing, and sincere friendship is one of the keys to unlocking greater contentment.

Brian, Seth, and Nate had begun to change that in me, to bring me out of a passive shell and into a proactive stance from which I would claim agency over my life and the growth I wanted. A more fulfilling life would be possible because those relationships pushed me into it. They pushed me into far more than my status quo could manage.

8

The Edge of the Cornfield

"The best preparation for loving the world at large, and loving it duly and wisely, is to cultivate an intimate friendship and affection towards those who are immediately about us."

JOHN HENRY NEWMAN

One summer during high school, Seth invited me to visit his hometown in rural southwest Iowa. Seth is one of those friends who has a knack for the spontaneous; he always pulls you into some adventure. Bob Goff was right when he said, "You become like the people you hang around, and to a great degree, you end up going wherever they're headed."[17]

Seth had scheduled an appointment to have his braces removed by the orthodontist, so he wanted to make a fun trip of it. We awoke before the sun came up that morning, swung by a truck stop to get unreasonably large cappuccinos, and blasted the car stereo all the way down the interstate and county highways.

After the orthodontist freed his jaws from the agony of wire and rubber bands, Seth showed me around the tiny farm town and introduced me to a few friends. That night, we'd planned to sleep on the living room floor of his friend Eric's house.

After the sun went down, Eric called some friends to meet up. They took us outside the town limits and parked between a towering red barn and the edge of a cornfield. Eric and the others brought instruments, camping chairs, and hearts full of song.

It only seemed strange for a passing moment until I felt I was really part of the group, and joined in singing songs familiar and new. They passed around the guitar and shared songs about girlfriends and bad days and Jesus, as if it was something they'd done a hundred times before, yet it held the authenticity of a simple community comfortable in its own skin. Friends don't need to plan much in advance; they can call each other up and determine a place. They simply go be themselves, loving each other and God, too.

I surveyed the dark, humid summer evening and looked up to a sky littered with the shards of a million brilliant stars suspended above endless cornfields. I sang to a God I was only beginning to know, even having known things about him throughout my upbringing. He seemed so deep and mysterious, yet near as the people next to me.

I was sure those friends in that cornfield were connected to the divine. And I wanted to be included in that sort of bond, with God and people all jumbled up together, taking on life like they knew each other and like they were going somewhere together.

These friends of Seth didn't see me as an outsider; they welcomed any friend of Seth's as one of their own.

That's something else a true friend does: he doesn't keep a friend to himself. He's got to share his friends with more friends who can be additional friends, because that's how an organic social network grows. It's not driven by popularity or status or selfish manipulation of others, but by the genuine pursuit of another human's wellbeing.

Friends don't need agendas or to make a detailed plan about everything they'll accomplish together; they just go do things. Healthy friendship gives and doesn't keep score, because it finds the equilibrium of give and take when people care about each other. Seasons change, and things may be lopsided for a time, but navigating these changes creates a powerful bond. These are the connections that impact our lives.

9

Curing Loneliness

*"What should young people do with their lives today? Many
things, obviously. But the most daring thing is to create stable
communities in which the terrible disease of loneliness can be cured."*

KURT VONNEGUT

I knew if I didn't make friends quickly after moving to Oregon,
I wouldn't survive. Staying in an empty apartment and wallowing in constant isolation would've driven me crazy.

When you taste the cool drink of authentic, encouraging
relationships, you don't want to leave the oasis you've found
because you fear it might turn out to be a mirage in the desert.

Minnesota

In my younger years, I was a rather adamant introvert. Social situations with new people or unfamiliar places were an
ongoing tension. I wondered if my quietness and desire to
spend time alone were weaknesses or character flaws to be
cured. Only after lots of time, and through humor and music,
would I eventually feel safe and open up to the few who became my friends. Even so, I felt ill-equipped to be fun and outgoing like my peers and adults in the classroom, church, and
social events. As author Susan Cain observed: "Extroversion
is an enormously appealing personality style, but we've turned

it into an oppressive standard to which most of us feel we must conform."[18]

When I went to college near Minneapolis, it taught me not just how to learn, but how to build a social life. No longer were my days scheduled with obligations I didn't care for. I could decide whether or not I would attend class, how late I would stay up, and which groups of people I would spend most of my time with. And in college, those I spent time with often impacted whether or not I attended class. Some days, my roommates—Brian and our friend, Daniel—and I would nearly convince each other to sleep in and skip class just because. Living two years in the campus dorms, we found that community was nearly built in.

Once I graduated college, my social sphere went through a hard reset. No longer were similarly minded people my age within walking distance, like the dorm rooms my friends and I used to drop by to share study materials and a few inside jokes. There were no more visits to the campus coffee shop where I was bound to see at least a couple familiar faces amidst the weekday morning bustle.

Social scenes after college were a smattering of continued friendships from the few people I knew from Minneapolis and old friends from high school. I was also learning to squeeze into the social circles those friends had already established back in my hometown.

Because of varying work and family schedules, it wasn't always convenient to see familiar friends. The impromptu runs to the late-night café and spur-of-the-moment dorm room visits were exchanged for miles between where we now lived and where we wanted to grab food or drinks. This transition produced a new kind of internal conflict with my expectations, and it taunted me with agonizing loneliness.

Still, moving back to my hometown after college provided a chance to reconnect with my family and some friends who had gone to universities out of state or found jobs in town. They made moving back home more bearable—especially nights watching movies or talking about nothing and everything with my friends. They made me laugh and have fun in the midst of my career frustration. It slowly became a refresher course in the importance of intentional relationships, a lesson I would desperately need in the years to follow.

Oregon

Since I didn't want to get lost in the friendship-less void threatening my new solo venture in Oregon, I took preemptive measures.

The weeks leading up to my move to the Pacific Northwest, I searched online for churches in Southern Oregon. I have to admit, I judged some of the churches by their websites—which, if you think about it, is really the new judging a book by its cover.

After picking a couple churches that looked promising, based on web design and belief statements that didn't make me cringe or cry, I sent e-mails introducing myself. I was moving to Oregon, I wrote, and I wanted to find some good roommates and a community group to plug into.

Only one church responded. A guy named Nick replied to my e-mail a few weeks later. He said he would love to meet me and see if the church could help me make some connections.

I read that e-mail again when my parents and I landed in Oregon, nervous to meet a stranger but eager for the chance to make friends. I would have laughed at you if you'd told me Nick would instantly become one of my best friends. And I would have rolled my eyes in disbelief if you'd told me he would be the one to officiate my wedding two years later.

We went to Nick's church the morning after we arrived in the Northwest. Mom diligently read the handout, while Dad surveyed the auditorium for someone who looked like he or she had an apartment for rent. After the Sunday service concluded, I walked outside to the crowded courtyard. The April sky was blue and beautiful, sunshine warmed my face and arms, and the hope for friendship beat through my chest.

Nick and I realized we were standing a few paces from each other in the courtyard. He was a bearded, tattooed, and gauged-ears guy in his late twenties who was built like a football player and listened to some of the same hardcore music I enjoyed. I was already grateful for the connection and glad he wasn't a weirdo.

Before my parents and I left for lunch, Nick invited me to meet some people the following Friday evening for a Bible study at his home. He and his wife, Katie, hosted it every week, and he said they kept it pretty simple with an acoustic guitar and group discussion. I took note and looked forward to the next weekend.

My mom and dad scheduled our week together: seeing the deep blues of Crater Lake; walking through towering redwoods; smelling ocean air on the California coastline just south of the Oregon border; and locating the most promising apartments and grocery stores in my new town. Saying goodbye to them that Friday was one of the most bittersweet days I've ever experienced. I nearly burst into tears driving away from the airport in the crisp spring sunshine. It was a make-or-break moment of conflict, with my head and my heart reaching opposite directions. *Focus on the future,* I told myself. There was a whole new chapter of my life to discover in the Rogue Valley— this corner of Oregon that felt like a foreign land.

Strangers

I gathered my composure and resolve in the hotel room before driving to the address Nick had given me for the Bible study. I parked a block away and walked intently down the long driveway. My inner introvert begged that I hesitate, but my yearning for community kept me walking right up to the open garage, filled with people my age around a ping-pong table. When things got started, I sat on the floor in a corner of the living room. About twenty of us looked around at each other between songs and discussion points.

I wasn't the only one there looking for community. Many of us, especially in the transient college and mid-twenties age range, desire more than surface-level introductions or niceties. Millennials are caricatured in news headlines and studies, but we felt then (and we feel now) what social researcher Brené Brown explains: "Connection is why we're here. We are hardwired to connect with others, it's what gives purpose and meaning to our lives, and without it there is suffering."[19]

All I was hoping for was a chance at a new story involving a few new faces—people to call friends who could know and understand me. This seemed like my one chance, the best time to make a real connection with a real person, lest I be resigned to my new life as a loner in a crowd—a self-induced, hopeless victim of social suffering.

The night began at seven o'clock and lasted a couple hours. Many lingered afterward to meet visitors and reconnect with the regulars. I talked with a few girls in the living room, then with Nick and a couple guys in the kitchen. Before I realized it, the clock read four in the morning.

I drove back to my hotel with a sense of gratitude, with high hopes that something meaningful had been started. After sleeping in that morning, I pulled out my computer and attempted to capture the feeling of the night before. This was the blog post I published:

Blog Post: Nine Hours with Strangers

Surreal. Unexpected. Yet, incredibly authentic.

They gather in rooms throughout a home, and sometimes meet in coffee shops, restaurants, and places around the city. Such variance in background, in life-happenings, in social connections, in spiritual journeys. *They gently surround and welcome newcomers as one of their own, just as if he or she had been a friend returning from a time apart.*

Welcome home.

The Father smiles at the sight of a room spilling with young adult life, couches and chairs and floors erupting with bodies that laugh and smile and sing and think deeply and challenge the superficial aspects of society. The Spirit says, "I love being here. These are my people. These are the ones I will change the world with."

They were the arms of God to me last night. They welcomed me in, befriended me, told me about pain in family life, about a new indie band's album releasing soon, about the history of where the winding road of life has brought us, about the best restaurants in town.

This I believe to be a great gift. This is Jesus saying, "I've got you here for something big and beautiful. And maybe they will be the ones you journey with. See, I've got people all over. Enjoy them. This is what church is about."

I was building a new life in a new home, and God had been up to something long before I arrived.

10

Dressed Up

"Let us be eager to leave what is familiar for what is true."
FRANCIS CHAN

Long before I got the call from a 541 area code, before I realized the courage required to step into the unfamiliar, my life was on a different trajectory—a far safer, more predictable one.

Average was an accurate description of my life: a middle-class family in middle America. Two parents, two siblings, and too much predictability. Most of my friends were just like me. We had the same kinds of clothes, the same haircuts, the same classes at school, and the same beliefs. I don't blame my family; I can hardly even blame myself. It was simply all I knew at the time.

Childhood treated us well. I felt stable in my family, safe and loved. My parents were very involved with me and my siblings—my older sister, Laura, and my younger brother, Lee. My mom and dad provided opportunities for us to try sports and music, and we got a good education. And because they knew the importance of being surrounded with good influences, they made sure my siblings and I were, too.

If the doors of the church building were open, my family was there. My parents made church a priority when they each became Christians in college, so it became part of our family culture.

Sunday mornings were always a production—mostly because my siblings and I preferred to pitch fits in staunch refusal to get dressed. Sunday nights at church were confusing: I was allowed to wear a T-shirt instead of a collared shirt, but the music and messages seemed no different than that morning's. Wednesday nights were the most difficult, probably because I couldn't reconcile my introversion with the large, awkward group games and the Bible memory quizzes that felt like another homework assignment I would never finish. Apparently, God demanded a lot from us even if we weren't all that interested.

My parents were supportive of our church activities and church friends. They also ensured we were well provided for and well protected. That's why we had pre-approved Christian magazines, curfews, and classical music.

I don't resent my parents for any of this. They did what they thought was best for us because they deeply loved us and wanted to prevent us from getting tied up in the wrong things. And for the most part, it worked.

Looking Good

One afternoon, when I was six or seven, I decided I wanted to see the heaven described to me by preachers and Sunday school teachers. My mom showed me how to pray about the things I'd done wrong and ask God to guide my life.

I wasn't sure what that meant, or how prayer worked, but I wanted to know more. Nevertheless, it was the beginning of something because faith is less about arriving at a conclusion and more about growing into a new way of living.

There was no turnaround in my behavior, nor a radical shift in my young awareness. It was difficult to see that I really needed to change because my life looked pretty good already. I was going to church and obeying my parents (usually). I tucked in my shirt and was nice to my friends, which seemed to be the gist of Christianity from what I saw. It wasn't until much later that I began to ask the questions I thought I already knew the answers to.

We were taught to act good because that's what Christians were supposed to act like. I never really questioned things as a kid; I just knew I was expected to play my part by going to church, hanging out with my church friends, and talking about church things. I learned how to play that role well. When I was old enough, I dutifully attended youth group on Wednesdays, relieved that I was no longer required to compete in Olympic-style games or wear a uniform that ranked my self-worth according to how many verses I could recite.

In the church I grew up in, everyone appeared to have it all together, so I assumed that was what normal looked like. Everyone had a comfortable, clean life, like I had a comfortable, clean life. There wasn't much conflict to worry about, unless you were too honest about how messed up part of your life was—then you had to worry about hiding that struggle. Smiles and positivity were hallmarks of every church service, and everyone wore his or her Sunday best as if a plaque by the door read, "No suit, no skirt, no service."

People would say they didn't believe it was a sin to go to the movies or play cards, but you'd get a lot of stares if they overheard you and your friends planning to play Texas Hold 'Em after you went to see the latest R-rated film. I wondered why there was a gap between what people said and what they really meant—and why were those things so bad in the first place?

There was one man named Lionel. Every church has a Lionel. My siblings and friends knew him as the elderly, furrow-browed man who yelled at us for running around in the darkened auditorium after Sunday night church services. Lionel scolded us for having fun "in the Lord's house." I was confused because when I heard about the God in the Bible, he was never angry about children hanging around him. Maybe Lionel thought God didn't like having energetic kids over because we were having fun but Lionel wasn't.

If God was like Lionel, I wasn't sure I wanted to spend much time around him. But I was fascinated by the character named Jesus, whom I'd heard a lot about in church and picture Bibles. He seemed so different than the people who attached his name to lectures and rules.

A Gradual Shift

When I was a freshman in high school, I learned to play three chords on an acoustic guitar. It opened up a whole world of musical possibilities, or, in Christian music, what seems like the entire catalog.

Because they were lenient or desperate for help—I'm not sure which—I was allowed to volunteer with my friends to be in a youth group band. Our band featured two acoustic guitars and a djembe hand drum, imitating the "contemporary" Christian rock singers and songwriters we admired. The youth pastor wanted us to share our musical passion, but the church leadership staunchly believed our choice of instruments and genres were best kept outside the church. They dismissed the idea as something for which the church wasn't yet ready. We were confused about why our eagerness to contribute was so quickly discarded. My friends and I wondered if our church would ever be ready for such a culturally progressive phenomenon known as percussion in the early 2000s.

More than anything, the rejection made me angry. I wanted to quit church because the dogma felt so stifling, so strict. But toward the end of high school, my new friends, Seth and Nate, invited me to their church's youth group—the same one my friend Brian had begun attending. The other church was not much different from the church I had grown up in, but it was different enough. They had guitars and bass and djembe, and even a full drum set. As far as I was concerned, they were in a whole other league.

Along with my chance to play more music, I reconsidered what I actually believed. I began readings books because I wanted to understand more about the world I lived in, beyond what I had always been told.

I began to question my own faith, some days more jaded than others. Rather than agreeing with everything I heard my parents or previous church talk about, I asked why. It wasn't so much about the existence of God, but why messages in which people used his name felt more like burdens than relief.

Most of the reservations I had were in the realm of practical living. Why did church and prayer matter so much? Who decided alcohol and rock and roll were so bad? "Who wants to live in an ivory tower when there is fresh air to breathe anyway?"[20] I wanted to know what difference my beliefs made on the actions of my life.

The new church was better than my parents' church, but it was still a set of checkboxes to live a good Christian life—evidence of who was in and who was out of line. By wielding the correct beliefs, I assumed the power of telling others what was right and what was wrong. And like before, I played the part outwardly while internally grappling with the sense that there had to be more.

Comfortable, sanitized, rule-bound religion destroys our thoughts, attitude, and perception of others. Jumping from one ideological rebellion to the next causes whiplash; you don't even know where you are anymore.

Snap judgments were my first impulse over giving people the benefit of the doubt. I thought I had God figured out. The pride of hiding my personal flaws became easier than admitting them. Somehow, my life was based on looking good to other people while putting them down, just like the legalism I had become appalled at.

I was a Christian who didn't listen to the Christ I professed. But that didn't stop him from trying to get my attention.

11

Little Things Are the Big Things

"To get these glorious works of God into yourself—
that's the thing; not to write about them!"

JOHN MUIR

When I first moved to the Northwest, I rented a room of a woman's ranch house, which was a lot less glamorous than it sounds. The nice thing about it was the seclusion it provided, nestled in the hilly countryside a few miles from town.

It was only the second week I had been in Oregon, still feeling alone because everyone I knew was thousands of miles away. I grabbed a Bible and sat by the window, facing horse pastures and the foothills of the nearby Cascade Mountains.

Journaling became the perfect escape from the pounding rhythm of my routine. It did wonders to close out of e-mail and silence the phone, settling into a quiet space with a view to read and reflect.

I gathered my thoughts and embraced the stillness, eager to post a new blog entry about what I was learning.

Blog Post: The Twenty-Third Refrain

Today is for thinking. Reminiscing. Daydreaming and resting and contemplating.

Eagles soar to and fro one hundred yards outside

my bedroom window, begging the bluest of skies to take them higher.

God is my shepherd. He takes care of everything I have ever needed.

His artistic canvas is the luscious green mountainscape I can see from my bed. His brushstroke is ten thousand gushing gallons of water amidst mossy wet rocks in the Rogue River Gorge. His paint is the snow-covered cap of Mount McLoughlin to the east of the highway on the way to town.

He has provided countless joys and moments of quiet confidence.

Even though seasons of life are dimmed beyond recognition of familiarity, whether facing troubles from your own doing or not, tread through the valley long enough and you will once again begin to climb the slopes of another hill.

"I will fear no evil, for you are with me."[21]

Little things remind me that there are such things as beauty, humor, and everything working just right in its own space.

Little things mean a lot, like the simple ambience of a coffee shop after a long week of overtime work. It's the right kind of relaxation in which to lounge with a steaming hot, dark roast and read a dozen pages of classic literature. Little things provide enough for a soul to drink in while the world pauses a bit.

"You prepare a table before me."[22]

Little things are the big things.

Little things keep us sane, keep us going, keep us mindful of the reality that things will be okay. Little things anoint us with oil, drench us with perspective. Little things can make our lives overflow with joy, like a Northwest spring rain.

"Surely your goodness and love will follow me all the days of my life."[23]
I want to dwell near that. I want to be around this, so that nothing happens without me being able to taste it and savor it.
"And I will dwell in the house of the Lord forever."[24]

In the Details

I stumbled into a truth that spring day: we can choose what to do with the little things we experience. Poet Maya Angelou said, "You may not control all the events that happen to you, but you can decide not to be reduced by them."[25] We may not control what happens to us, but our response determines the way we let events impact us, for better or worse.

We often want God to convince us of his reliability. But really, the whole time we're getting lost in the little details and wondering where God is, he's in the same place, waiting for us to come to our senses and remember he actually loves being found in things little and big.

A beautiful thing about the Bible is that it's ancient words full of timeless truth. Though Psalm 23 was written thousands of years ago, God still says to us today, *I will take care of you. Don't worry about the big things. Enjoy the good amidst the little things.*

12

Sunday School Liar

"Be interesting, be enthusiastic, and don't talk too much."
NORMAN VINCENT PEALE

Eleven-year-old John was a liar.

I don't remember if it was a pattern, but I do recall one horrific transgression in particular.

The rotund, cheery Sunday school teacher was talking about a Bible story in which some characters had to go days without food. He was probably referring to the Israelites wandering the desert for forty years or Jesus in the wilderness. He asked the class if we'd ever gone a day without eating food. As the seats were filled with mostly middle- and upper-class suburbanite children, no one raised a hand.

Except for me.

For some reason, eleven-year-old John decided the moment was ripe for the picking. I told the class of my family's recent vacation to the western wilderness of Colorado or Wyoming. I crafted a quick tale of our experience sitting in our cabin, nestled among the pine forests and rocky terrain, without food.

The only problem with that account is that it never happened. Out of some desperate plea for attention, sympathy, or some other self-serving motivation, I plucked a story out of thin air. I lied.

I'm sure the Sunday school teacher must have recognized

my misappropriation of the truth. How could a middle-class student have been in such dire straights on a family vacation? It seems so juvenile and silly, completely unnecessary.

As a good little Christian boy, I was well aware of the ninth commandment: "You shall not give false testimony against your neighbor."[26] I didn't know what my neighbors had to do with it, but my brazen wrongdoing shocked even me. We ate every day of family vacation, and I never had to go hungry unless I chose to avoid food of my own volition. So why did I lie?

The Small World of Self-Promotion

There's something about the human heart that flirts with the edge of morality. A drive for self-promotion, comfort, security, or fulfilling a personal desire even drowns out rationality at times.

We've all got embarrassing stories and foolish mishaps from the days of our youth, or even more recently. No matter how hard we try or how far we've come, ego encroaches on our more noble aspirations. Every choice we make about the truth brings its own kind of conflict, whether internal wrestling matches or external consequences. *Give me recognition; I deserve some attention, it says. Regardless of the cost, I want it.*

Those are dangerous thoughts—ones that weasel their way into our subconscious and actually make us believe we're the center of the universe. It's a tricky thing to keep that self-promoting ego in check, to keep from wallowing in self-defeat but still maintain a healthy perspective of both our good and bad traits.

Self-analysis can take us only so far because we are not all we should be about. We're meant to get past immature self-promotion and look beyond ourselves to the beauty of the world, to aid those around us. Life is too big to be selfish, too grand to waste it on ourselves.

I imagine I kept quiet the next week at Sunday school, enough to keep others from remembering the previous week's fiction. Hemingway said writers need a built-in BS detector[27], but I had discovered an ability to be a BS creator. Perhaps I should have known I would come to love stories and the telling of them. There it was, a preconception in my young mind that the typical details were far too small when more exciting stories could be found beyond the ordinary.

13

Saved from Mediocrity

*"If Jesus exists, he don't live in the pages we write. He'd say,
'Put down your books and come follow me out in the light.'"*

PETER BRADLEY ADAMS

When you begin to challenge your assumptions after being stuck in a world of black and white, you can't help but see more and more grey. Part of me felt required to act like a good person and avoid the uncomfortable questions, but I couldn't ignore them anymore. The internal wrestling match had already begun, and I needed to find God on my own terms.

At the end of high school, fraternal support from Brian, Seth, and Nate anchored me in the midst of all the questions. Maybe God wasn't the stoic, distant being I had previously supposed.

I started to see how the Bible wasn't a weapon to use against people, but medicine for the sick, even if I didn't know how it all worked. God didn't desire rigid rule-followers, but attentive friends. "If Christians have learned anything from our rocky two-thousand-year theological history, it's that we make the most beautiful things ugly when we try to systematize mystery."[28]

I knew a lot about God from growing up in church, but I felt as if I wasn't useful. I wanted the coach to put me in the game, to get some real playing time on the court. In the Bible, when Jesus befriended people who weren't well liked, or when he spoke about the value of serving others instead of expecting to be served[29]—those were the things I needed to do with my own hands and heart. Sincere faith must move from observation to action. Instead of listening to more messages and spending more time in a church building, I was compelled to put knowledge into practice.

The Other Church

My senior year of high school, I told my parents I was going to stop attending their church and get involved in the other church, the one that believed in drums. I wanted to contribute in a place that actually liked guitars. As I became more involved, someone asked if I would join the band for Sunday services. It was like being called up to the Big Leagues, but I still hesitated. I really had no excuse since I'd left my former church for the purpose of greater usefulness at the new one.

My involvement didn't stop with music. The youth pastor asked me to co-lead a Bible study with Seth for a bunch of middle school boys. There was a sort of fear hidden in the back of my mind, that these boys would hear all the things we told them but none of it would impact them—that the way they acted wouldn't be changed, even though we were helping them see there was more to life than girls, sports, and standardized tests. I didn't want them to be like me, little Pharisees with flip phones and directionless lives. Real learning and maturity are products of time and experience, but I wanted them to grow up instantly.

That thinking was more a reflection on my own immaturity than anything. I would easily grow frustrated with the boys' lack of interest in the Bible and talking about God. The frustration was grounded in my fears that young guys would waste their lives in the mediocrity I felt I was failing to escape. My own view of God wasn't big enough to handle when people casually walked away from him. I had yet to learn that God's timeline is far more baffling, but it is always better.

That year was a major turning point of my life, though not dramatic or obvious. I was facing the small conflicts that required me to adapt, so I could prepare for bigger conflicts later on. Things were changing and I was okay with it. I even welcomed the change, which seemed like a huge step forward in itself. I thought it was what growing up was supposed to be like: a slow but steady hike up a mountain with its peak in the clouds. The view may be obstructed, and I may not be able to see what's around the curve of the path, but at least I was walking uphill.

Making a Path

There's an old Spanish proverb that says: "Traveler, there is no path. The path must be forged as you walk."[30]

Though some days I'm not creative or bold enough to leave the familiar path, I know I'm headed somewhere and doing something.

God is in the business of putting people on a new path. It's a familiar place for him, too, because he goes with us as we walk. He must enjoy seeing us navigate the trail this way and that, avoiding pitfalls and cliffs. Even when we get lost in the tall grass, he's eager to call us back on course.

When God put me on a new path, it was one away from the stifled, functional legalism I lived within. Some days it's especially apparent he is still calling me away from mediocrity. The whole thing is a process. On a new path, it's more rewarding to ask questions than to spout off answers I previously assumed were correct. That leaves a lot more question marks, but the ambiguity is less scary and more rejuvenating than the dead end of preconceived notions.

I'm grateful God didn't give up on the former person I

was. He's exercised endless patience with young, rebellious, half-hearted boys like me. Even as adults, we revert back to our timid, misguided, and selfish inner children, but he invites us to a new path. It's a work of God that we're able to change at all. God wants to improve us, to make us better versions of ourselves, what writers of the Bible called "perfect" and "holy."[31] I don't exactly know what a perfect life looks like, but I know I'm far from it. I get the sense his ways are right and true and beautiful ways to live, and sometimes I cringe when I realize the ways I've run the other direction from that compelling life. Perhaps it's a sign he's still working on me, like I'm an athlete realizing what his body can accomplish if trained and disciplined.

The Bible even uses sports analogies to describe the journey of life. The early church leader Paul, nearing the end of his life, said, "I have fought the good fight, I have finished the race, I have kept the faith."[32]

I don't know what the rest of my path will look like, or even what the next steps will be, but I know God has promised to be with me on the trail, through the change and conflict, just as he's always been. And that gives me hope that my life will amount to something, that it won't be a waste if I'm keeping pace with the author of life and of my story.

MOVEMENT TWO

Disruption

14

Seeing the Invisible

"When you believe in community, you contribute your life."
JEFF SHINABARGER

A month after I started my new job in Oregon, I found a room-mate and moved my things from the room in the countryside to the new apartment in town. Packing up my things didn't take long those days. Everything I owned fit into my blue Honda sedan.

There's a sort of freedom in not possessing too many material goods, in the lack of ties to physical objects. I almost felt like a Franciscan monk, detaching myself from the world's measure of success.

Securing an apartment and a roommate felt like I was firmly planting myself in a new chapter, making progress in this variable life I pursued. Though a relatively small feat, it felt like an accomplishment. Like different scenes contribute to one movie, different places provide context for relationships to develop. Hanging out with friends and building a community needed a space, somewhere to live and breathe and grow. The apartment provided that space. No matter where you are with friends, what matters most is that you're there together.

A couple phrases ran through my mind during those days. Amidst change and variables and the unfamiliar, I clutched at any truths I discovered like a swimmer gasping for air between breaststrokes. God carried me along on this unpredictable story, and each chapter revealed something I needed to know for a future moment of need.

I grabbed my journal to record my thoughts, then typed up a new blog post to share.

Blog Post: Fragility, Friends, and the Invisible

Where we are isn't so important as what we are doing there.

What we have isn't so important as who we journey with.

It seems like the less trappings of life we concern ourselves with, the more we are freed to value things that can't be held, touched, or seen. Temporary things are easily visible, and eternal things seem invisible.

Things that really matter are made of both soul and matter.

Life is not easy; at least it's not meant to be. An easy existence with no substantial conflict makes for a lousy story. Our lives are like stories, cut out of pages and sewn together in three dimensions. Whenever our lives are void of conflict, the danger of indifference sets in. Where there is nothing to achieve or no battle to fight, there is a weakness of will. A muscle lacking exercise gives way to atrophy.

Some people I know shared about the jobs they've lost unfairly and the relationships they wish were in better times. They're in the midst of situations that inflict personal discord. And they're in need of resolute will to face the conflict, to know who they are in the heat of battle.

Relationships are messy. People lie.

Careers are disrupted. Families are broken apart.

Hearts are stung. Trust is betrayed.

Especially because I'm a newcomer to the circle of friends, I find it easy to make excuses not to get involved in their struggles. Fortunately, God is more patient with me than I am with other people. I'm grateful he sends people to help other people, and at times, I'm the one who needs help facing conflict.

Things that really matter are made of both soul and matter.

Temporary things are easily visible. Eternal things dance on the line between visibility and invisibility.

We are all fragile.

We all lack answers.

We all face conflicts, because that is the stuff of living.

The inevitable conflicts of life find us each in our own time; so when they do, may we be found beside one another, securing each other for the fight.

Where we are isn't so important as what we are doing there.

What we have isn't so important as who we journey with.

Rich Moments

I am still learning how to channel my attention to fight for my friends, not with them.

It's easy to leave people at arm's length to deal with their own problems. If I'm powerless to change anything about their situation, why bother? But God doesn't leave us to address our problems alone. The times I've needed it most, he's provided people to surround me.

Honesty and proximity are the noble challenges of a good relationship:

You'll miss the richest moments in life—the sacred moments when we feel God's grace and presence through the actual faces and hands of the people we love—if you're too scared or too ashamed to open the door.[33]

I hope you've felt that, too. It's a powerful thing to have a shoulder to cry on and a heart to confide in—the unparalleled expression of God's presence through other people.

15

The Electrical Soil

*"Music is the electrical soil in which the spirit
lives, thinks, and invents."*

LUDWIG VAN BEETHOVEN

All of us reach turning points.

At some moment in our lives, we realize we don't really want to do what we thought we wanted to do, so we step onto a new path. We cast seed onto different land, hoping something takes root. The seasons change and the earth warms up, nutrients buzzing into new life.

Music was my turning point.

During middle school, I would smuggle a pocket radio and string headphones through my shirt so my parents didn't know I was listening to Top 40 radio while I practiced shots on our neighbor's basketball court. Back then, my mom and dad weren't particularly fond of the idea of pumping distinctly non-Christian messages into our inquisitive minds. I wanted to be a good Christian son, but those drumbeats and pop hooks were just so enthralling. I had to hear more of this forbidden fruit.

When I joined my middle school's basketball team, I instantly loved the road trip experience of away games. My friends would bring their Discmans and swap CDs to listen to each other's collections of pop hits from the late 1990s. Returning to our hometown one night in a packed fifteen-passenger van was my first luxurious opportunity to listen to whole albums, a smattering of heathen rock and pop, without my parents around. Forbidden music was my drug, and its allure followed me into high school.

Music drove me further into isolation as I got lost in my introvert world, but it also drew me into community. I abandoned sports for melodies and rhythm, which brightened into the center of my focus. The same was true for my closest friends.

Punks

Brian and I formed a band with another friend, Derrick, writing and playing punk rock in our parents' garages and calling ourselves Total Capacity. Derrick was tall with wavy blond hair, and he taught himself to play bass. He always sported the nonchalant, trendy punk look so well—that's why I copied his style choices as best I could: tight T-shirts, Chuck Taylor All-Stars, grungy jeans, and disheveled hair. Seth joined the band for a while because I wanted to step back from lead vocals so I could play guitar riffs more accurately. (Whether my playing improved is another story.) In the spring, we played our first and last gig with Seth as our frontman.

After our performance, Seth said he didn't feel he had the "it" factor. We also took note that he still preferred his pastel polo shirt collection to our random thrift store T-shirts. The band continued once more as a trio.

As we grew older, our musical tastes matured. When I say *matured*, I mean that we preferred increasingly aggressive and angsty-sounding arrangements. From the punk rock scene, we ventured into hardcore, screamo, and metal. To match our evolving tastes, we hatched the idea to disband our now-insufficient punk ensemble to create a new five-piece band.

Music gave us the foundation we needed to grow into

something new, something different. It became part of our identities and helped us express who we were and who we wanted to become. Our passion was the kernel, and music was the electrical soil that awakened our zeal to create things that mattered to other people. Maybe it was God providing the metaphorical sunshine and rain, just enough reason for us to burst out of our previous shells of comfort so we could produce art instead of just consuming it.

The music meant a lot to us, even if it was typical punk rock or abrasive hardcore to outsider ears. It felt like we were creating soundtracks for our lives, narrating the seasons of teenage frustrations we'd been through and anticipating the future of college and adult life with nervous excitement.

Screamers

Nate joined as the lead singer and additional guitarist. At the church Nate and Seth attended was our friend DQ Dave, who got his nickname because he worked at the local Dairy Queen when they first met him. DQ Dave was a few years older than us—bearded and tattooed with gauged ears and a lip ring. He fit our desired image perfectly. We all wanted tattoos and piercings, but we hadn't quite made it to 18 (or calmed our parents' reservations on the subject).

DQ Dave was the band's screaming vocalist, juxtaposing Nate's lead melodies with a hardcore edge, just like our favorite bands that used two vocalists for the sing/scream routine.

We stayed up late in the church's auditorium to practice new songs. With this new roster and intensified sonic change, we performed a couple concerts at real venues under a new, more hardcore emo band name: Answers for the Broken Hearted.

We were miraculously booked to play two nights in a row. We called it our first "tour" because the shows were in two different cities. The first night, in our hometown, we packed the small venue. Getting in front of our friends and tuning up our guitars made us feel like real rock stars. I think a couple people even sang along and hardcore-danced, or did something between headbanging and starting a lawnmower.

The next night, in a nearby town's venue, Derrick and I—without prior planning—swung our guitars around our torsos at the exact same pause before a breakdown and the crowd of a few dozen teenagers went wild. (At least I think they did.)

Reinvented

When Nate moved to Minneapolis to finish his bachelor's degree and Brian departed for college on the East Coast, we disbanded. Since our heavy ensemble had crumbled, finding other ways to play music was only natural.

It was my senior year of high school when I joined Seth and our friend, Bruce, at their church to play acoustic guitar with their band. The music had taken a drastic turn for the more palatable, but I was okay with it. I still cranked up my amplifier and stereo to jump around to heavy music in my bedroom, longing for the day I could be in another rock band, touring the country with my closest friends and seeing a different skyline every night.

Adapting

There is a time and place for the dreams we cultivate. The trick is to know what's in line with the real trajectory of our lives and what would lead us off course. These transitions are supposed to be part of our journey. "The actual way that we change is we experience a disruption. We hear something that grabs us and we can't go on in the same way."[34]

Disruption produces conflict that forces us to adapt. In that way, disruption helps us improvise and improve.

Over the years, we all grow into a phase and hopefully out of it, then into a new season. It is the way of life to change and transfer from one state into another. Our desires and convictions and priorities change. It is how we know we're maturing into healthier, wiser people who learn from our experiences. If we haven't grown out of something, how can we be prepared for more of life down the road?

Change is a constant; the way we embrace transitions makes all the difference. Even the transitions themselves can enrich our lives if only we let them. Our variable lives make more sense the further we go, gaining the perspective hindsight offers and allowing us to mark the course we've been traveling.

16

Middle School Romance

"To love is to risk not being loved in return. To hope is to risk pain. To try is to risk failure, but risk must be taken because the greatest hazard in life is to risk nothing."

LEO F. BUSCAGLIA

Love was an elusive creature for me early on.

It must have been seventh grade when I pondered what I thought could be a serious love story with a cute girl in my class named Valerie. I daydreamed about how we would be the most adored couple at the small private school we attended. All the boys wanted to be with Valerie, brunette and fun and smart, so it was impossible for me to tell anyone else I liked her. Love triangles have a way of freezing the vitality out of junior high friendships like Minnesota Februaries wick away any warmth from one's multilayered attempts to prevent cold toes and fingers. Yet "nothing makes us so lonely as our secrets,"[35] so I had to do something about it.

Attempt #1

One spring afternoon, after months of internal debate and wistful longing for requited love, the time seemed right. My mother was soon returning from my siblings' after-school activities, and my father was still at work, providing the privacy the moment deserved. I summoned enough courage to grab the school's phone directory and nervously pace the living room with cordless phone in hand, deciding on what tactful wording would best convince Valerie we belonged together.

I dialed the number a couple times before actually connecting long enough to hear the first ring. I felt the pangs of love against my weakening resolve.

Two rings. My palms were clammy with sweat. Three rings. Someone picked up on the other end. I feared my heartbeat would cause my speech to stutter.

I gulped and nearly hung up. Once I confirmed it was Valerie on the line, our conversation was brief.

"There's something I've wanted to tell you for a long time."

"Okay..."

"Um, I like you."

Silence.

"I just thought you should know." Silence.

I attempted to elicit a response. Anything. "So, I'll see you at school?"

"Okay, bye," she offered, hurriedly.

The isolation of silence enveloped the room; I stood frozen with sweat-covered phone in hand and a quickly closed phone directory. Adrenaline spurred me to ditch the evidence and look busy doing something when my mother and siblings returned a few minutes later.

Nothing seemed different with Valerie at school the next day, or on the following days. Perhaps the only change was she avoided me a little more than before, but I didn't notice. I didn't want to notice anything that would deflate my crush, but I was still curious where she stood with the burgeoning passion we were supposed to share.

The ambiguity carried on, as did the close of the academic year. Summer passed, and eighth grade dragged on while I tried to focus on basketball and being liked by my classmates, avoiding situations that reminded me how I failed with Valerie. The first week of June, a year older—but not wiser—my teenage self still wished for some sign of reciprocated affection from Valerie. Everyone in our eighth-grade class was invited to someone's house for an end-of-school pool party. This, I thought, would provide the perfect opportunity to clarify my romantic intentions and, once and for all, win a girlfriend before high school.

Attempt #2

The day of the pool party arrived. We all ate ice cream cake, swam in the pool, and made funny faces as we invented dives off the springboard. The sun was going down, and the event was nearing its end, so in a desperate attempt to incite Valerie's curiosity, I nonchalantly mentioned she should see me before the night was over because I had something to tell her.

The nonchalance was essential. I'm not sure it came across that way, but it was certainly what I hoped to project as a cool and easygoing eighth-grade graduate (because every middle school kid knows it's not cool to try too hard). I didn't want to seem desperate—interested, yes, but not pitiful and desperate.

I stuffed my towel and swim shorts into my backpack and passed a wistful goodbye to the remaining few classmates and Valerie, hoping to heaven she'd remember my conversational bait before my dad picked me up. As I wandered from the backyard pool through the house to the front door, I felt as if my chances of love were evaporating like the long school year had: unfulfilled, unresolved.

The sun set behind the trees as I sat on the driveway, contemplating the close of the day and the beginning of summer break in Minnesota. My heart skipped a beat when I heard Valerie's voice as she bounded out the front door to sit beside me on the driveway. This was the moment I had been waiting for, alone with the girl who evaded my romance once before. I knew my time was short so I cut to the chase, palms sweaty as before.

"I still like you. And I want to know if you like me, too."

Silence in person was worse than on the phone. I could see her face freeze with a look of surprise and quick mental processing. Her swimsuit dripped on the concrete. The breeze danced in my hair. My eyebrows raised in anticipation of a response. Anything.

"Well, um...I like someone else."

It was my turn to pause in silence.

"Oh."

Deflation.

The moment swelled with sudden awkwardness. "Have a good summer!"

With her farewell, she ran back into the fortress of the house, denying me any chance to offer rationalizations why I would make a better boyfriend than her mystery crush.

A cool evening breeze rustled the trees across the street. I stared at the stars appearing in the darkened sky. I waited for what seemed like hours, alone on the driveway with the puddle beside me—until it evaporated, too.

When my dad finally picked me up, the car ride home dragged on, streetlight after streetlight passing while I stared through the passenger window of the Chevrolet. I didn't want to talk. My despair built a wall of isolation, convincing me no one else would understand the heartache of my misplaced love.

There was little chance I'd see her around anymore. We were attending separate high schools in the fall. I couldn't decide if that was a good thing or a bad thing, because for a while, I still thought I could win her affections: denial, repression, cross-examination, depression.

My excitement for the summer had all but disappeared. Three months of freedom from school became a dreadful, barren wasteland. I lost a sense of purpose for days and weeks. I knew the feeling of heartbreak was supposed to pass eventually, but I didn't want it to. I wanted to mire in sorrow. I wanted closure, but not like that. Love wasn't supposed to be so conflicting.

Love Lessons

It was all very silly, the way we middle school children bounced around, declaring crushes and hoping for a real dating relationship when we were barely in our teen years. Perhaps it's a rite of passage, enabling young minds and hearts to grow accustomed to what becomes a primary concern in the stage of adulthood. Maybe the throes of middle school love serve as a warning, preparing us for a world that often deflates the most hopeful among us, leaving us out to dry like a puddle on the driveway.

Looking back on high school and even in college, dating was over-dramatized—simultaneously treated too haphazardly and too seriously. It's a practice that deserves discernment, maturity, and calculated realism instead of purely emotional, ungrounded desire.

Failed romances made me a calculated risk-taker. I learned to analyze and wait longer to act—usually not out of maturity, but out of a fear of making the wrong choice. That's how you avoid getting hurt. Yet love always includes conflict; you can't avoid it. When I think about taking relational risks, now I measure them up against the maturity I hope I've gained and the wisdom of my past experiences.

When done well, calculated risk-taking and love go hand in hand. The method I've found helpful is something I call *The John Weirick Slow Play*. That approach could fill a whole book on its own.

We must be willing to risk if we want to find love that's

shared, not just received. Risks are required if we hope to experience anything of lasting value. So maybe in some small way, that summer after middle school, I was preparing for the circumstances I didn't know I would find myself in when I started a new life in Oregon.

17

Meeting the Girl

*"Love is an ever-changing, complicated, choose-your-own adventure
narrative that offers the world but guarantees nothing."*

DONALD MILLER

My first Thanksgiving in Oregon sat juxtaposed against the
classic Midwestern Thanksgivings of my childhood. I slept
until the middle of the afternoon—due to working overnight
shifts at the radio company—and didn't watch any football.
A couple families I knew opened their homes to some of the
twentysomethings who no longer lived near their parents, so
I was privileged with the opportunity to eat two Thanksgiving
dinners. And I was invited with some other friends to eat dessert at a girl's house.

The Girl

One of the people I'd met at Nick's Bible study in Oregon was
a girl named Kati. I'd liked her honest friendliness, the passion
she'd shown about living a life that made a difference, and her
boldness in speaking about things that mattered to her. Early on, I'd noticed her humble elegance and how she'd laughed
with a brilliant smile. Stunning blue eyes hid behind her wavy,
dark brown hair.

I didn't move to Oregon with the intent of meeting a girl. But when I saw Kati across the room and heard her speak thoughtfully about what God and the Bible had to do with real life, it didn't sound like a theory to her; it sounded like a living, meaningful practice. I knew I had to get to know her.

Over a few weeks in the spring, I noticed Kati at some of the group's events, and I was a little sad when she left for the summer. But as soon as she returned in the fall, I wondered more about her. We crossed paths occasionally and spent time with mutual friends, and I liked it. I liked her.

By Thanksgiving, I had been interested in Kati for a few months. Her family invited a few friends over for dessert and, to my surprise, she extended an invitation to me. So before going in for my overnight shift, I stopped by Kati's parents' house for coffee and pie.

I walked up the steep driveway, a little nervous but anxious to see another dimension of Kati's life. She often talked about how much she loved her family, so this was a chance to see her in a natural environment, around people who mattered to her most.

She answered the door and introduced me to her parents, sister, niece, and friends around the room. Over dark coffee and pumpkin pie, we exchanged a few remarks about work, family, and mutual friends. Before long, I had to depart for that familiar, unwelcome battle against my better judgment: the overnight shift.

Though a simple hour or two, that evening of pie and coffee reinforced my curiosity about Kati and began a foundation for my relationships with her family and friends.

Cautious Attraction

We wandered through that undefined territory between friendship and mutual interest. It's a mysterious, uncertain landscape, leaving you unsure about where it leads and whether your next step will be on solid ground or quicksand. Maybe that's what makes romance exciting.

As fall became winter, we grew to understand a little more of one another and caught glimpses of what brought life and what incurred frustration for each other. We posed curious questions about personality and worldview, listening closely when sharing stories about past pains and important moments. Over a dozen or so meetings for local coffee, while hiking rocky trails in the shadows of the Cascades, and during casual Friday dinners before we went to Nick's Bible studies, our friendship grew more comfortable, and our hearts grew fonder.

We were careful—I didn't want to rock the boat. It seemed important to maintain a healthy realism about each other. From the start, neither of us wanted dramatic friendships that turned into flings that turned into broken hearts. We'd each known the frustration of unhealthy and rushed relationships in previous years. Neither of us wanted that again. Kati and I didn't set out to be a romantic couple; it was more about seeing a person full of kindness and conviction, who followed Jesus and marveled at amazing things. I just wanted to be around her. She was the kind of woman I wanted to spend my life with: beautiful, adventurous, learning to be independent and humble.

I dated a few girls in high school and college, but it was toward the end of college that I actually considered what I really wanted in a partner, if one at all. As I watched married couples I knew, observed adventurous love in action, and read about marriage and relationships, I found myself hoping not just for a romantic significant other, but a companion in all areas of life.

The Beginning of Romance

The Bible's account of the first man and woman is rather poetic. It carries so much evocative beauty, whether you read it literally or figuratively. I imagine the expression on Man's face as he looked into the eyes of Woman, the partner God crafted from a deep nap and spare rib.[36]

Earlier in the story, Man named all of the animals in the Garden of Eden, but found none of them appealing. He noticed none of the animals were designed to be his match. So as soon as Man awoke to see his new friend, something so profound stirred in him that he burst into verse. Some consider it the first song in the Bible, a love ballad expressing the attraction and connection he felt toward this mysterious yet familiar Woman.[37]

Love manifests in alluring ways. An inward yearning for intimacy, commitment, and companionship blossoms into sincere affection toward an individual, whether reciprocated or not. To feel love is to know you're alive. It calls you to something deeper—to pursue a meaning that goes beyond reason or logic. One counselor says:

> All of us must face our fear of rejection, be healed of shame, and risk our hearts in relationships. We must be willing to offer the truth of who we are to those we love, and receive the truth of who they are. Only the truth can make us free.[38]

All of our truth about love is rooted in who God has been to us.

The Thrill of the Slow Play

There is no better way to use the past than to learn from it. Analytical introspection—like any self-respecting adamant introvert would tell you—often distracted me, but usually clarified what I really wanted and how I would go about it. It would be easy to use a girl to have a good time, but my conscience would haunt me. A better story would be one with adventure, humor, and depth—a partner I could call my best friend.

Rich friendships are proven through shared conflict and joy, built slowly over a long time. If I were to find romance with one who could be my best friend, I would have to build on the foundation of friendship from the beginning.

So I enacted *The John Weirick Slow Play*. The *Slow Play* is the development of a relationship that moves from establishing friendship toward romantic involvement, but stays free from romantic expectations. Perhaps if we minimized the social pressures often associated with the dating scene, we would get a better sense of who the person across the table really is. *The John Weirick Slow Play* provided me the space to be Kati's friend without leaping into hastily contrived dating right away.

The best of romances can blossom from the deepest of friendships. The *Slow Play* wasn't about the game of romance or the thrill of the hunt; it was about enjoying the process of friendship, in all its patience and authenticity. Every relationship includes conflict, but I wanted to avoid the unnecessary parts as early as possible.

Creating the space of an unlabeled relationship without romantic expectations allowed us to become really good friends. And through that friendship, we realized just how compatible we could be. I wanted to minimize the chance of hurt and heartache that a breakup would inevitably include. Kati deserved better than that.

Sometimes caution holds us back too much, but it's a worthy consideration when a person's heart is involved. Calculated risk-taking opens our eyes to reality so we're best prepared for what comes next.

Love is always a risk, and I was beginning to think I was ready for it.

18

In the Wilderness

"An inconvenience is an adventure wrongly considered."
G. K. CHESTERTON

It was my Uncle Mark who introduced me to fly fishing. After he bought me a rod and reel, I spent hours casting in the backyard.

He took me out to the lake a few weeks later. Uncle Mark wore waders up to his chest, a fisherman's hat with a short, upturned brim, and a sly smile beneath his mustache—a true northern outdoorsman. I wore old sneakers, dirty jeans, and an inquisitive look, though I was grateful for a new adventure. We each found what we hoped to be promising spots along the shoreline and stood in our respective places for an hour or two—Mark wading in the shallows and me staying on land. Long after I had given up hope of catching anything, I hooked a seven-inch bluegill. We brought it to my parents' house, and he filleted it in the front yard so we could eat the meager portions for dinner.

Uncle Mark is always eager to get out of the bustling city noise and into the wild. He taught my siblings and me how to navigate canoes down the Zumbro River, steering with the paddle dipped off the stern. When I was a teenager, he stopped by one day and took me out to a remote forest road to teach me how to drive stick shift in his 1980s Jeep. I took a few road trips with him to Northern Minnesota, where we lodged in frigid cabins and stayed up late making snacks around the campfire. He listened to the natural world, a remnant of generations past that lived out in the woods and told stories dense with trees, animals, and untouched landscapes.

He's cut from the same cloth as explorers like John Muir, who said, "Take a course in good water and air; and in the eternal youth of Nature you may renew your own. Go quietly, alone; no harm will befall you."[39] Mark embodied Edward Abbey's conviction:

> Wilderness is not a luxury but a necessity of the human spirit, and as vital to our lives as water and good bread. A civilization which destroys what little remains of the wild, the spare, the original, is cutting itself off from its origins and betraying the principle of civilization itself.[40]

The woods beckon him often, lush riverbanks offering solace, the simplicity of open sky his inspiration and window to the God he knows and loves. Mark's love for God is blatant as the sunrise. He talks about God like they walk through the forest together, and I believe it.

Uncle Mark took solo trips to the Boundary Waters Canoe Area every year. During the 300 miles driving straight north and exploring the millions of acres of wilderness and hundreds of lakes, Mark takes nothing more than basic supplies for camping, canoeing, eating, and fishing. It's not a fishing expedition, a vacation, or a time to get to know other outdoorsmen.

Mark calls this tradition his alone time with God. And he says that God speaks to him every time. Uncle Mark's not one of those people who hears God in every raindrop and fallen leaf, but he recognizes God's masterpiece of the natural world. His vision is tuned to the majesty of the creator's complex beauty and simple truths.

Unexpected Exodus

Not long ago, my family sat around the dinner table enthralled with one of Uncle Mark's tales. He told the story of his most recent trip to the Boundary Waters for alone time with God. He was a few days into the trip during one of the coldest Mays in Minnesota's history. A phantom cold spell drifted through the Northland earlier in the month, leaving ice and snow longer than expected. Many of the lakes still had floating ice pads splashing against each other along his canoe route. He'd been to the wilderness area dozens of times before, but this year was not his typical alone time with God.

Nevertheless, Mark's determination pressed him further into the wilderness, alone and enjoying the time away. After several hours of sleep on the fourth night, he suddenly awoke at 4:00 a.m. without explanation. He sensed God telling him to pack up and get out of the Boundary Waters. Mark asked God if his wife, Anna, was okay, and God said yes. Mark asked if his kids and their families were okay, and God said they were. Mark knew it was time for action, but he didn't know why.

Uncle Mark rolled out of his sleeping bag and began tearing down his campsite under the pre-dawn sky. The stillness of the early morning shifted as light rain fell and he prepared a quick breakfast. As light broke, Mark saw the darkness of storm clouds approaching from afar. He hastened his packing and shoved off in the canoe to cross the ice-littered lakes once again.

As the trek continued, Mark kept wondering why God was telling him to get out of the Boundary Waters. He considered his physical condition: vulnerable rotator cuffs, a canoe with limited capabilities in icy water, a sixty-pound pack, and more distance to traverse than he was accustomed to in a short amount of time. Normally, he paddled through lakes and passed two or three portages in a day—several hours of strenuous work.

If he were to make it out of the Boundary Waters by the end of this day, he'd have to pass through seven portages, sustaining upper-body strength while repeatedly hoisting up a canoe to carry on his shoulders.

Mark asked again if God was sure he needed to get out of the wilderness that day. God said yes, so Mark bolstered his courage and made way through the lake and portage and onward.

Midway through his urgent race, Mark relaxed his paddling pace and told God he wanted to do a bit of fishing. He cast a line in hopes that this particular area held up to its reputation as a good fishing spot. After several unsuccessful casts, Mark inquired, "I'm not really supposed to be doing this, am I?"

Onward Mark went, passing campsites on lake's edge filled with puzzled looks on the faces of other campers, who remarked at the rapid pace Mark sustained across the water. At one point, another solo camper invited Mark to shore with the offer of food. After a quick bite, Mark explained his urgent mission, and bade the man farewell.

Uncle Mark finally made it through the last portage and lake as dusk approached. He paddled the canoe to the rocky shore, pulled it up out of the water, and strapped on his pack for what he thought would be an easy hitchhike nine miles down the road to where his car was parked.

After several minutes waiting beside the road, Mark wondered if God was still insistent upon his directions to leave. If no vehicles were present to offer him a lift to his car, Mark would have to hike the whole way. Several moments passed and Mark decided he'd better get moving, so step after weary step, he urged his exhausted body forward. He didn't walk the road back angry with God for the painful, taxing journey his day had entailed. In his own deliberate way, Mark started down the road, singing hymns and reveling in the grace of making it so far.

It was two and a half hours later when Mark reached his vehicle and drove it back the nine miles he'd just trekked to retrieve the canoe. He stepped out and stared at it, realizing the severe strain his back had already undergone in the day's seven portages. Would he be able to lift the old 17-foot canoe above his head and slide it onto the Jeep?

Mark spoke candidly with God: "I know you've gotten me this far. My energy's shot. You're gonna have to get this canoe on the car."

A moment's repose, then with the full remaining measure of his upper-body strength, Mark heaved the canoe across the top of the Jeep and strapped it down for the drive home. Relief flooded his mind as he climbed into the driver's seat, though his weakened legs were so sore it became difficult to press the clutch and accelerator pedals.

When Mark drove into Ely, the small Minnesota town that served as a main launching point for Boundary Waters expeditions, he called Anna and asked if she was okay. She told him she was, as were their kids and their families. Mark told Anna he'd had quite a day, and unfolded the story of God's directive to leave the area immediately.

After concluding their phone conversation, Mark reclined in the driver's seat, with the Jeep sitting in a campground's parking lot, too fatigued to care about setting up a tent. It was late and the journey long—fifteen hours and many miles of traversing the Minnesota wild were behind him.

That night, exhausted from the astounding trek, Mark lay in his car and asked God, "Is there a particular reason you told me to do that?"

Mark chuckled when God answered, *Is there a particular reason you're asking?*

Revelations

As Uncle Mark concluded his story around the dinner table, he smiled reminiscently, proof he didn't regret that day one bit.

Although it was one of the most physically demanding things he'd ever done, it was also one of his sweetest times of communion with God.

Mark still doesn't know why God told him to leave the Boundary Waters in one day, but he's looking forward to the next time he'll journey into alone time with the one who leads and sustains.

I am learning to hear God's voice like my Uncle Mark does. I wonder how our lives would change if we got away from our routines more often. "No wilderness, no revelations," Susan Cain warned us.[41] The freedom and peace we might find away from smartphone notifications and incessant schedules could create the space we need to take one step further into the life God sets before us.

19

Getting Out of Safe Mode

"Does anyone ever realize life while they live it, every minute?"
"No. Saints and poets maybe."

THORNTON WILDER, *OUR TOWN*

My Uncle Mark's experience in the wilderness caused me to rethink my approach—whether I insist upon the comfortable consistency of my own choices or listen to the wild call of a mysterious, untamed God.

It would be a lot easier to follow God if he didn't insist on such difficult things. The Bible records God saying a lot of things that come off confusing, if not illogical and a little embarrassing. Christians hold beliefs that seem really strange when considered from an outsider's perspective. I don't know about you, but I've never heard of anyone who decided to become a Christian when she heard about animal species marching seven by seven into a big boat, when people groups were slaughtered, or when Jesus told people to eat his flesh and drink his blood.[42] Those sound weird, horrific, and repulsive.

God's followers have a long history of being ashamed of him and disobeying his instructions. Story after story is filled with imperfect, messy, self-righteous, judgmental, immature, fearful, and wayward characters God repeatedly pursues until they quit running away from him and simply embrace him as they are. Even after all that, some still go their own way.

I don't think God wants us to understand everything about him, or to simply memorize facts or pillars of spiritual truth we can spout off at a moment's notice. He's after our friendship. He'd rather know us and teach us to know him. In knowing him, we find our purpose and our source of living. We find the love and truth we've been searching for once we give in to God's embrace. Saint Augustine said it like this:

> To praise you is the desire of man, a little piece of your creation. You stir man to take pleasure in praising you, because you have made us for yourself, and our heart is restless until it rests in you.[43]

God lets us experience discomfort so he can move us toward something better. When we're comfortable, we put down roots and plant ourselves in a current situation, relationship, or job. We build a routine, a schedule to provide us security and consistency. Avoiding or ignoring conflicts now impedes our ability to navigate them later. It enables us to coast because we know what follows the next thing, and the thing after that. When we know what's next, we don't need to trust in anything but ourselves.

In this way, comfort can distort into idolatry. A job becomes a career becomes a god we place ahead of God. A relationship becomes a lover becomes a spouse becomes an idol we treasure more than the one who gives value and faithful love. Good things become idols when we replace God with what we want. Our own unchecked desires usurp the throne, our lives devolving into rebellious overthrow.

If we hold tightly to God, loosening our grip on ease and comfort, we find ourselves adaptable. We're empowered to handle whatever circumstances come our way, because our maker walks with us. When we orient our lives around the God who made us and knows what's best for us, life opens up into the freedom of adventure, risk, and purpose. It's not just an existence; we're meant to really live.

A friend once said his fear is that the comfort and security of home will one day replace the longing for adventure of the unknown. He doesn't want to settle. He wants to stay flexible, adapting as he trusts God through the uncertain variables of life.

Escaping comfort and living adventurously with God reminds me of something Seth wrote in his journal on a trip to Oregon. He shared this with me a few years ago:

Seth's Journal Entry: Reflect, Record, and Meditate

As I sit in the observation car on an Amtrak train bound for Klamath Falls, on a sunny Oregon afternoon, I feel as if I should record my thoughts and observations about this adventure I'm having.

Although I have pictures from this trip, I probably won't remember the intricate details about the simple yet amazing things that have made this trip what it is. I thought about this in the context of my life. I have snapshot memories, but forget the intricate details along the way. In contemplating all the things that make me who I am, I fear that in not taking the time to reflect, record, and meditate, I have lost an opportunity to grow—both spiritually and as a man.

In college I took a canoe trip to this wonderful secluded wilderness called the Boundary Waters. I did it through a college course my second year of community college. We were instructed to keep a journal—the only graded component of the class trip—a detailed log of our activities over the five days in the wilderness. I got a C on the journal because my notes weren't practical. My professor said something about me needing more specifics so that on future trips I could find my way back to these campsites and good fishing spots. He had recommended practical reflection and recording so on future journeys I would know the best way. I would know from my previous experience and errors what to do and what not to do.

This is an image of my life. I need to take the time to reflect, record, and meditate on the simple details of my daily journey so on future journeys I will know what to do and what not to do. I'm tired of living a mundane and lazy Christian life. I know from this trip that I long for adventure and that part of me has an untamed spirit. But I also know I am too much of a rational thinker sometimes. This leads to what I call safe mode.

Like a computer, I am most free from risk when I boot in safe mode. But I need to take risks. I don't know what those risks might be, but I need to live a better story.

In these adventures I find solace. I discover myself more and realize my place in this vast universe. I realize God is great and has created so many people I love to meet and strike up conversation with, but I want to actually love them enough to take the risk to share Christ with them. My desire to do this is there, but I have to kick it out of safe mode.

I haven't quite figured it all out at this point in my journey. But I know this: I must reflect, record, and meditate to grow.

Transforming Conflict

Seth is on to something.

We don't grow unless we are faced with a challenge. A smooth sea never made a skilled sailor.[44] A threatening force compels us to rise to a higher level to confront it. Outside of our comfortable routines, we're forced to adapt to the new conflicts we've previously been sheltered from.

By facing conflict, our lives take on greater meaning. We're all meant to play a role in something bigger. Many find something bigger in a cause, attaining wealth or power, or exercising dominance through aggression for a particular value, like the warriors of an ancient (or modern) culture defending its people and principles.

Individuals leave civilian life to sign up for military service or volunteer abroad because they seek these rites of passage. They want to experience something that proves they've moved from one phase of life to another. Author Steven Pressfield describes this in his book, *The Warrior Ethos*:

> We're seeking some force that will hurl us out of our going-nowhere lives and into the real world, into genuine hazard and risk. We want to be part of something greater than ourselves, something we can be proud of. And we want to come out of the process as different (and better) people than we were when we went in. We want to be men, not boys. We want to be women, not girls.[45]

Conflict reveals and refines. The way we face adversity shows who we really are, and it helps us become more deeply who we are. In the wasteland of testing, we learn about the story we're living and how we can make each plot twist count. Outside our comfortable, status quo existence, we find a world urging us not just to survive, but flourish.

In the frigid wilderness, Uncle Mark sensed the depth of God's presence and patience. In the stillness of reflection, Seth realized the rewarding possibilities buried within risky exploration beyond the boundaries of safety. In the flames of adversity, we are refined into more mature renderings of the people we are meant to be.

The world is big, beautiful, and dangerous, but we have access to something bigger. God stands out in the forest, hands open toward us. He awaits our company on an adventure to change us and clarify our vision. Saying yes to the adventure is how we prepare for what's next.

20

The Lost Get Found

"It is not the healthy who need a doctor, but the sick."
JESUS

We naturally get uncomfortable around people who are not like us. Moving to Oregon was especially difficult—those first few months of awkward conversations, assumptions, and misunderstandings.

The larger the differences seem to be, the more inclined I am to avoid interaction with someone. I have become very adept at navigating away from the conversations most likely to produce awkwardness. If someone approaches me and I characterize this person as one who will not likely communicate on my wavelength, I will avoid him or her. And I will avoid situations centered around subjects with which I am neither familiar nor interested.

As every introvert knows, people are too much work.

It's a cowardly, fear-based method of thinking. Introverts aren't always wrong to avoid people—there are legitimate reasons to draw clear boundaries and protect solitude. Yet other times, though we don't like to admit we're wrong, we take the easy way out. Being patient or kind requires social and emotional energy, but it offers no guaranteed benefit. Our instinct is to reject the remote possibility of something valuable down the road, even if we cognitively know that operating out of fear rather than love is no way to live. Operating out of fear cripples our sense of connection and our capacity to love.

Love From a Distance

Differences keep us distant if we let them.

The distance isn't just a geographic one, but also a social one, besieging us into claustrophobic worlds of isolation. The separation begins out of something small, inconsequential even, but it grows if left unchecked. Separation results from misunderstanding, from a lack of common bond. Lies and deceit are the seeds of mistrust, planted with unaddressed grievances and unresolved conflicts.

This sort of social distance keeps once-dear relatives away from holiday reunions, or keeps old friends bitter from an event in their past. Separation even hinders us from opening up and making new connections. Human beings so often fail one another.

I know I've got a long way to go when it comes to sincere love. One writer in the Bible put it this way: "There is no fear in love. But perfect love drives out fear, because fear has to do with punishment. The one who fears is not made perfect in love."[46]

It's when I make conscious efforts to step out of my comfort zone while maintaining the confidence of who I am that I'm freed to connect, love, and engage those who may be, in a sense, far from me. Love can't show up without humble effort. Ideas won't be explored. Connection won't occur. I read this in a book the other day: "Conflict becomes dangerously ugly when we react out of fear and pain. Fear feeds conflict because it is in every way opposed to connection."[47]

God knows many of us who claim allegiance to him neglect people deemed too different. Laziness, misguided priorities, and apathy plague the church. We're all as disconnected from each other as everyone else.

One of the most beautiful things about Jesus is that he shows us what it looks like to engage with people who are different from us, even those we consider too far from God. The whole story of the Bible centers around this: God connected with people who were far from him, spent lots of time with those people, and told those people to connect with more people. Jesus offers us an escape from social selfishness to explore the freedom of shared life. We are made for connection with God and connection with others.

This is the retracing of our steps from the separation sickness we've contracted. It's practically impossible to love from a distance. God designed us for community. He calls us out of our dark, isolated corners to gather under his light, together with him and with more people.

We're all in a story, and stories intersect—at least good ones do. Engaging in those connections, especially the dissimilar ones, is part of what makes the story great. Maybe authentic connections and community can grow from the smallest of seeds to a forest of trees if we see that God's way is to bring together what's different.

Maybe through these relationships, the story can become about redemption, reconciliation, renewed life, and second chances. Together, burdens can be carried, tears streamed, and joys celebrated. People are too much work, and they are too much reward. Through these shared experiences, we can learn how the Gospel changes us for the better: the good news of a God who cares enough about people that he goes on a search-and-rescue mission to bring them together in the light.

No longer alone, no longer unloved. This is how the lost get found.

21

Private School

"Youth cannot know how age thinks and feels. But old men are guilty if they forget what it was to be young."

J. K. ROWLING

There were a lot of things I didn't understand about my school, an institution that prided itself on offering a classical Christian education. My siblings—Laura and Lee—and I attended from elementary to middle school. It felt like a private Catholic school, except it was Protestant and had far fewer relics and symbols— but we did have rules, punishment, and our own sort of liturgy.

All 150 students, kindergarten through 12th grade, frolicked across campus in our mandatory pleated khakis and blue-and-white polo shirts, but we didn't really know why we had to wear what we did. We were told wearing uniforms helped us focus better on our schoolwork because we'd spend less time comparing our clothes with those of differing socioeconomic backgrounds, and it was less likely someone would wear an inappropriate outfit or a bad word on a T-shirt. (T-shirts sounded fun.)

Every month, a certain Friday was designated as "Mufti Day," the meaning of which I'm still not sure. It sounds like we were supposed to act like hoodlums and dress like ragamuffins. By bringing a dollar, each student was allowed to ditch the uniform and wear normal clothes as if we attended a public school—although administrators still looked down on questionable T-shirt language and too much skin above or below the torso. The funds could've been used to fund school dances, concerts, or sports tournaments, but they probably just went to something boring like operating costs.

Mufti Day was the coolest day of each month. To a young, burgeoning mind, normal clothes in school were a loosening of the shackles of rigid academia. No longer were we bound up in ugly, faded yellow or navy blue polo shirts with boring khaki slacks. Most of the girls in my class were relieved to accessorize something other than plaid jumpers.

I pushed the figurative buttons of my eighth grade algebra teacher, Mr. Mohler. The class had learned his first name—Jacob—and he did not share my sense of humor when I addressed him by it during classroom questions and answers. His firm, collected response spoke louder than his words.

Between parabolas and integers, he frequently told us about his love of surfing and home in Hawaii. He was young, composed, and approachable, often brushing aside his wavy dark hair and adjusting his glasses for a better look at the whiteboard. His quiet confidence felt like friendliness in a school where students loved few teachers. I may have hated math, but at least there was something relatable about Mr. Mohler.

He gave me hope that not all Christian educators were more interested in students keeping rules than in helping us grow as people, though some teachers did their best to reinforce the stereotype. Mr. Mohler created a classroom environment that not only welcomed us, but also helped us see that learning and fun were not mutually exclusive. Questions and tangents served as guides, not distractions. The tasks of academia were valuable, but Mr. Mohler invited curiosity that pulled us into life lessons beyond a rigid syllabus.

It's hard to justify learning just for the sake of stiff, memorized facts. Learning for the sake of an unfolding world is something to benefit eager minds as they seek a life of purpose and meaning.

The Last Day of Eighth Grade

The last day of school that year was ripe with optimism. Final tests had been taken, desks and lockers cleaned out, and a school-wide water war was scheduled for after lunch. Unbelievable summer bliss permeated the sunshine-filled Minnesota air.

My posse filled the tanks of our Super Soaker water guns and stuffed our pockets with spongy water bombs. Plans were hatched to divert attention away from the centrally located water hoses, our only source for reloading. Younger schoolmates were separated between the four or five huge teams, and the Battle of the School Lawn commenced.

I mostly looked for my brother so I could ambush him. We chased the girls we had crushes on throughout the year. I simultaneously wanted to clearly avoid and defiantly confront Valerie amidst the screaming underclassmen. As the water combat proceeded, the warm sun hid behind cloud cover, rendering cold, wet projectiles all the more devastating. It was a battle of epic proportions, and many soaking wet schoolchildren sank to their knees in drenched defeat.

That final day of middle school also held special reverence among my peers. The newest installment of the *Star Wars* prequels had been released that month. Opening showings of the films offered sacred appeal for wide-eyed teenage boys. It shouldn't have been surprising to our parents, then, when a handful of my friends asked permission to leave early on the last day of school to see an afternoon showing of *Star Wars*. After all, we were only missing the aftermath and cleanup of the water fight.

As we piled into my friend's mother's minivan, Principal

Sharrow approached the vehicle. His long strides from across the parking lot seemed foreboding, just like his rigidly thin frame, grayish-brown eyebrows, and hard-soled Oxford shoes. As the last of us buckled in, Principal Sharrow poked his head in the doorway of the van with a mild smirk.

"Where are you guys going? The school day isn't over yet."

A few of us made humorous quips about the greatness of *Star Wars* and offered excuses for our early departure. "It's the opening week!"

"There's nothing else to do. School's over."

Principal Sharrow shot a glance to my friend's mother, who smiled pleasantly, fully aware that the remainder of the afternoon's activities held no academic value whatsoever.

"Who said you could leave early?" asked Principal Sharrow, unimpressed.

"Don't you like *Star Wars*?" retorted one of my friends.

He must have acknowledged our enthusiasm or remembered the celebratory nature of the last day of school. Maybe it was a combination of both. In a show of humanity and goodwill, Principal Sharrow turned to the rest of us with a wave goodbye.

"Well, don't do this again—but have a good time. Enjoy your summer!"

We rode out of the parking lot with a feeling of closure, leaving behind another year of school and the foibles of junior high education. No more would we look up to high schoolers or sense our inferiority in the academic caste system. Onward to a magical summer of unreasonably high expectations and upward to the next chapter: high school.

Things were looking up.

The Life You Choose

I suppose the structured, independent part of me always wants to maintain control of what I do and when I do it. The impulse to find my own way and experience the world on my own terms undoubtedly tainted my perception of Principal Sharrow. He was trying to maintain some semblance of academic rigor at a school that had a reputation to uphold, but my peers and I were too intent on pushing the boundaries of the world we knew.

Our childhood years leave impressions on us, whether the experiences were good or bad, strong or weak. That summer still stands in my memories as one that held great potential for change, like my life was building up excitement for the future I was walking toward. I couldn't put it into words, but I was gaining momentum by learning to become my own person. It was a subtle but necessary conflict that required my attention. Each year, it got a little bit easier to make decisions without needing the approval of my peers or adults. I grew more comfortable being me.

Making choices and dealing with the consequences is part of growing up. Author Cheryl Strayed wrote:

> I'll never know, and neither will you, of the life you don't choose. We'll only know that whatever that sister life was, it was important and beautiful and not ours. It was the ghost ship that didn't carry us. There's nothing to do but salute it from the shore.[48]

Sometimes, we just need to stand up for our own decisions, regardless of how someone might react. Sometimes, we just need to skip the last day of school to watch *Star Wars*.

22

The Marks of a Servant

"Relationships are never about power, and one way to avoid the will to power is to choose to limit oneself—to serve."

WILLIAM PAUL YOUNG

As a young teenager, I never considered that body modification could hold any meaning or beauty. In gas stations and grocery stores, I stared at peculiar facial piercings and unsightly ink markings across portions of strangers' skin. I had no idea why anyone would want such an unnatural item lodged on his or her body for any length of time, let alone a lifetime.

My perception of tattoos and piercings morphed when I was in high school. As my friends and I moved away from light-hearted rock into punk and hardcore, we noticed the kind of style worn by the artists of the scene. Clean-cut and plainly dressed weren't good enough anymore. To be a true fan of the music, we subconsciously reasoned, we had to dress the part. Image was everything, second only to actually playing music.

Dress the part we did, and the more obscure the T-shirt, the better. After all, punk rockers didn't care; they weren't supposed to care about anything except the boldness of their cultural rebellion and the blistering tempo of the newest punk song.

As we grew into the angsty hardcore and metal genres, a solid half of our T-shirt collections became tight and black. Then our attention turned to the hair, the holes stretched in fleshy earlobes, and the prominent tattoos that would be barely covered by aforementioned black T-shirts.

Long before any of us actually got tattoos or piercings, we eagerly planned where we'd get matching nautical stars inked on our bodies. Of chief concern was which kind of piercings looked the most hardcore. We lived divided lives—part in the dream world of being in a hit punk band, and part in the reality of school and chores.

We transitioned from our pop-punk trio into a screaming, heavy five-piece band. We would tune our guitars and check our microphones while taking note of every person in the crowd with full-sleeve tats or big, stretched ears from double-zero gauges. The more ink and metal someone wore, the more credibility we attributed to him or her. The more we saw our idols look a certain way, the stronger we felt compelled to imitate their style of clothing and accessories.

We become like whatever holds our attention.

An Ancient Tradition

Later in my senior year of high school, I learned about a different sort of body modification, not just the kind for appearance. I discovered the story of the ancient practice of bondservants: the dedication to lifelong service in the same household.

Before we go further, I need you to know something. This is an uncomfortable story to tell because there's so much baggage connected to terms like "slave" and "bondservant." The risk of misunderstanding is high, but I believe there's something valuable to be gained if we carefully evaluate what the story means.

Parts of the Bible describe slavery as a part of civilizations, economics, and common life in the ancient world. God didn't prescribe slavery; the writers of the Bible simply acknowledged it was part of history and the world they lived in.

We often hear "slavery" and think of U.S. history a couple

hundred years ago, but there were different kinds of slavery throughout history. There's nothing okay with owning another human being. God doesn't condone oppression and dehumanization in these passages, but creates a way for those who would normally be kept poor and marginalized in the ancient Middle East to find protection, provision, and blessings. Bible professor Preston Sprinkle wrote about Old Testament customs:

> This is the world Israel lived in. To exist, they had to take part in these structures while at the same time critiquing them. And this is what the law of Moses did. It didn't outlaw every less-than-perfect cultural practice; rather, the law took the practice as it was and improved it.[49]

Just as God provided for the Hebrews when they were set free from slavery in Egypt, God made a way for Israel's slaves—whether native or foreign—to become part of the family of his people. With that in mind, let's get into the story.

According to ancient Hebrew culture recorded in the Bible, men and women who found themselves in debt or obligation to another person would become that person's servant.[50] At the end of six years of completed work, the head of the house was to offer the servant the chance to leave the household in freedom, even lavishly supplying him or her with parting gifts. However, some servants had grown accustomed to life serving the family of the house or had married another servant there.

In the event the servant wanted to stay with that household after completing the six years, the head of the home would take the servant to the doorpost of the house. He would split or pierce through the servant's ear with an awl, symbolically binding him or her to the home. The servant became a bondservant, bonded or belonging to the same family for life. From that day forward, the bondservant wore an earring as a symbol that he or she had found a place to belong in that family and would willingly serve them.

God took something people used to mistreat and exploit each other, and he turned it into a way to include people in something better. God didn't approve of slavery, but he worked through an imperfect, conflicted system to bring about a new and beautiful change.

This ancient practice resonated with me. I remembered a verse: "You are not your own; you were bought at a price. Therefore honor God with your bodies."[51]

The way the Bible explains things can be a little odd or complex at times, but God never communicates without intention. One thing the ancient world understood well was that the first humans didn't appear out of nowhere. Humanity was born from the divine. Scripture paints a poetic and graceful picture of our humble beginnings, of the creator reaching down into the dirt and forming Man, and then grasping Man's side to form Woman.[52]

From the beginning of the world, everything belonged to God. Everything in our solar system and galaxies beyond, down to the cells of our DNA, exists because of God's creative ambition. Creation implies intent, for no maker makes something complex and beautiful without purposing it for specific tasks.

God is my maker and my origin; I don't belong to myself. In the same way, you are not your own. I don't know what you think about God, or what he made you for, but I think he made you for something.

Alternative Perspective

One passage in the Bible describes Jesus as "the author and finisher of our faith."[53] He's a cosmic writer, drafting a story with you as a cast member. And he won't cut your role, either; he intends to finish what he started with you. No matter where we're at, he's not the kind of maker who discards his work; he tends to put what he made on display.

It's when we abandon God's ideas in our search for purpose that we lose our true identity. If we separate from the one who designed and created us, we stray from the life we're intended to live. We're like wayward bondservants who have left the household in search of something different, but we realize nothing else welcomes us like the family we belong to.

When a bondservant committed to serving a household for the rest of his life, he was saying he'd found his place. The family became his, and he became an adopted part of their lives for the long haul. The family's kindness may have led them to grant the bondservant partial ownership in the family's land or business. No longer an outsider merely working a job, the bondservant had a new, redefined status and future—from slave to son or daughter, an heir to the inheritance. And that's how God describes us.[54]

That wasn't just an ancient custom; it became a way to make sense of my story. I wasn't just a high school punk trying to fit into the style of the scene. Yes, I wanted tattoos and piercings and I thought they looked cool, but because of that story, there was another meaning in those things calling out to me.

Like a kind head of the household, God invites us to stop trying to hustle and prove our way into the family. He already offers a place at the table, a home in which to belong. Jesus invites us to something better, urging us to set down our selfishness and enjoy him and his people. God is a father who invites the undeserving like us into the family, to experience its benefits and dignity. We have a new future and a new way of belonging.

I wanted to remember my new identity, who I was and who I belonged to. That story ran through my mind as I sat in a Minneapolis tattoo parlor and a man with more piercings than I had fingers to count pushed needles through my earlobes and slid my first earrings into place.

23

What God Wants

*"The quality of your commitments will
determine the course of your life."*

RALPH MARSTON

It wasn't long after I moved to Oregon that my new life set-
tled into a weary rut. The same day, the same routine, the same
commute to work and back. The lunches were different, but
the tasks continued, unchanging. Day after day of work, then
returning home when the sky faded, weeks bleeding together
in the mundane routines that swallowed the hours. Darkness
set in as I wheeled the garbage bin down the driveway, and the
same darkness lifted as I halfheartedly rolled that bin back to
the house before work.

Some seasons of life are like trying to fit together the wrong
puzzle pieces: they just don't match. Adventurous yearnings
and a drive to accomplish something meaningful are unsettled
in the labyrinth of routine.

How do I figure out life? Is this all there is to being an adult?
Will I have to follow the routines and obligations society sets
before me, or do I get to choose my own course? I know I'm
not alone in posing the questions. Many of us—my twenty- and
thirtysomething peers—are especially curious for answers.

It's not always spoken in so many words, but it's obvious if
you read between the lines: we want to know that this life is

worth its struggles. Is there more than the internal conflict of wanting something better but fearing we're missing out on it?

We're known for posting incoherent, ambiguous, and self-centered updates on social media, like "FML" and "first-world problems," and we forget the arrogance on which that attitude is built. On a global scale, Americans are well within the top five percent of wealthiest people. If someone in the United States earns a modest five-figure annual salary, he or she is among the top one-percent wealthiest in the world.[55] Skip around to see how a few other countries are doing, and we'll see they're still struggling just to get reliable, clean water.

I don't bring this up to shame those of us who are wealthy Westerners, but to remind us that much has been given to us and much is required of us.[56]

Finding God's Will

Many of the friends I made in Oregon are navigating their twenties, that profoundly defining period of life. They're at the doorstep of this universe of opportunity, yet they often become frozen with all the choices before them. Nick calls it "the paralysis of analysis." With so much time and resources, options emerge everywhere. Opportunity allows us to seize the moments before us and wrestle them into something tangible. The Digital Age is fertile soil for the bumper crop of jobs, networking, and relationships. Opportunity is in season, and it's so ripe.

For Christians, choices among endless opportunities are compounded by another seemingly impossible question: what is God's will? What should I do with my life? Whom should I marry? Whom should my friends be? Where should I live, and how will I get there? And how will I find the answers?

These are questions my friends ask, the ones blogs and magazines pose, the ones pastors preach about—sometimes too tritely for my analytical nature. The concerns are valid ones, because life is composed of such questions, but I wonder if we're missing the point.

The God my friends talk about is big and powerful, yet gentle. He's outside of time and space, yet he has jumped into moments and places to encounter people who've asked the same kinds of questions since humanity's humble origins. We bring our questions and concerns, and he responds with answers or reframes the question in a verbal dance—as if we're pen pals, but cosmic and intimate all at the same time. Haven't we all yearned for clear, concise replies from the heavens—just the answers we want, not the ones he usually gives us?

He speaks to us so often, but we've got so many distractions and other ideas pleading for our attention. Silence and tranquil listening are the endangered species of the Digital Age. Maybe if we'd more deliberately pause our modern technological frivolities, we could sit down and have a talk with God about what it is he wants us to do with our lives.

Many nights during the first year I lived in Oregon, I sat on the back porch under dim lights with the sounds of nature and distant traffic blending into a solacing soundtrack. After a day of work, busyness, and activity, it was good to unplug from the world. It's often how I reconnect with God and with myself, a deep exhale after the hurried breaths of routine.

A lot of those porch times, I asked God why—why something bad had happened to my friend, why I had to wait for some sort of resolution, why I couldn't fix something that was grating on my conscience. And sometimes I asked him about the circumstances or trajectory of my life.

God's will for every detail of my life wasn't dropped in my lap, shouted like marching orders, or sent in the mail. I'm glad if that's your story, but it's not mine. Over the course of a few years, God kept on making calls to see what I was doing, and he invited me to hang out with his friends. I went through stages of liking his friends and then feeling disconnected from them, but he kept on telling me it was okay and I should hang on for a little longer. He had something more in store.

Growing up in a family of Christians, I developed a cursory knowledge of God and a bunch of the things he said and did in the Bible. But the more I took God seriously for myself, the more I discovered his personality and his ideas, and the more I got the sense of what he really wanted of me. He didn't tell me all of his will, but he told me enough. He tells us all enough, in the times we need it.

It's God's will for everyone that we learn to love each other, despite the nasty things we've done and the grudges we've held. And it's also God's will that we use what he's given us. Jesus talked about God being a good dad who gives his kids what they really need, and sometimes what they want, even if they're snotty nosed and annoying.[57]

Because of God's generosity toward us, he provides everything we need. When we shift from living out our own will to living out God's will, we change the way we use what God's given us. It's a stewardship role: it all belongs to him, but we're taking care of it for a while.

Do What You Want

If God has given us the energy and ability to accomplish something, we're responsible to use it. If we've been given certain abilities or a specific burning passion, we should pay attention to that. It's like flipping over puzzle pieces to see how the colors and patterns align. An expansive ocean piece won't fit next to a bright orange fire hydrant. God probably won't tell you to be a secluded, remote forest ranger if you're an extrovert, passionate about being with people all the time. But if he wants you to do that, he'll make it pretty obvious. A limitless God has a way of doing what seems impossible to our limited perspectives.

There's a popular quote from Saint Augustine, who lived around AD 300 and wrote books that people still read today. In a sermon about love, Augustine is credited with saying something astounding: "Love God and do whatever you please."[58]

At first glance, the phrase could be easily misconstrued and selfishly applied. But here's the second half: "...for the soul trained in love to God will do nothing to offend the one who is beloved."

God doesn't want us to dwell in the paralysis of analysis, all caught up in the tiny details of every choice. That sort of thinking just creates a sticky web of excuses if the conditions fail to align perfectly. "Love God and do whatever you please" is about sticking with the God who made us and looks out for us. And as we keep in stride with him, we can do what we are passionate about, using the skills that come naturally for us and are supernaturally enhanced by God.

If we walk with the one who made us, we learn who he's made us to be. "People function at their peak when they function out of identity."[59] God whispers in our ears, as we keep pursuing the dreams hidden in our souls, *This is my will. It makes me glad to see you work this out, because this is what you're made for.*

24

Down on the Farm

*"Opportunity is missed by most people because
it is dressed in overalls and looks like work."*

THOMAS EDISON

The summer after I graduated high school, I worked on a cattle ranch. I'd held a profound respect for cowboys since childhood, so I was delighted at the opportunity to be one, technically speaking.

Some friends of my family lived in rural Southern Minnesota on 330 acres of rolling green hills covered with fields and forests. My siblings and I had gone to school with their children, so we were all well acquainted. I asked the family's father for a job in the spring, and he said he could put me to work as a part-time ranch hand. I called him Boss from that day forward.

Three days a week I drove out to the farm, and three other days a week I worked in town, stocking shelves at a department store. That summer kept me busier than I had ever been, with only a brief day to rest before the other six days struck again.

It felt good to perform manual labor in the open air. Most days, I worked with the family's son, Patrick, who was a few years younger than me but far more knowledgeable about farm life. And there was Jake, another friend of the family, who was about Patrick's age and worked with us a couple times a week. I was taller than both of them, but they were stronger than me.

Our tasks often centered on keeping the hundred or so cattle watered and fed, which meant we moved them to a new hay-field every few days.

At noon, Patrick, Jake, and I would drive the ATV up to the house for lunch that Boss's wife, Erika—who had the brightest smile and the most joyful disposition—prepared for us each day. The family had built the house a few years prior, and it was a thing of beauty. It sat atop the hill, at the end of the windy gravel driveway that connected to the main road. We could sip lemonade on the porch and see miles of green farmland stretch around us.

Boss always seemed to care deeply about the land, the cattle, and how they did things on the farm. He often surveyed the land, watching the animals in stillness and then adjusting his baseball cap and glasses before he walked to the next pasture, muck boots gulping through the sticky mud. All the cattle were organic grass-fed, and I could taste a difference when Boss gave me some steaks to take home. It tasted fresh, like wild game, as if the bulls had been grazing wild in their natural habitat. I suppose that's the way Boss wanted it, as natural as could be. Boss and Erika prayed for us before we headed back out to the fields each afternoon. They saw the land and animals as gifts from God, and they treated them as such. I grew a deep respect for Boss and his family that summer, like he was a modern version of the thoughtful, kind, hard-working cowboys of the Old West.

Caring for the Land

When there are 330 acres of farmland, rows upon rows of fence line keep the cattle grazing in the correct fields. Endless rows of fence line meant lots of weed whacking—one of my main tasks on the farm. When the grass grew too tall, it brushed against the electric fences and sapped the power. So every few weeks, we'd rotate to different fields to trim along the fence.

One July afternoon, Patrick, Jake, and I were out in the far back fields weed whacking fence lines. The sky grew dark and cloudy as we approached the final fence to trim. The three of us were spaced about fifty yards apart, motors whirring against the knee-high hay when rain began to fall. We looked across at each other and picked up the pace. It wasn't long before thunder rumbled in the distance and then lightning flashed across the sky. We exchanged one last apprehensive glance and hurriedly finished the final trims as the raindrops grew larger and thunder shook the ground.

We loaded onto the ATV and flew back to the barn, giddy with excitement and pleased with our accomplishment. We raced into the house to dry off and watched from wide living room windows as sheets of rain descended. Thunder boomed over the lush greens and browns of fertile Minnesota, reminding us we could only do so much work on a farm, but God always knew what the land needed and he provided it.

Learning to Try

I learned how to drive a tractor on that farmland, moving massive round hay bales into rows and raking lines into the brush and soil. My stick shift tractor driving was barely passable, so the rows were more like zigzags. If the work proves the craftsman, as the old German proverb goes,[60] I was far from skilled— but at least I was learning to try.

Some afternoons, while driving the tractor in the far field, I would use headphones under soundproof earmuffs, wear my faded black baseball cap, and take off my shirt to attempt to get a suntan. I enjoyed the seclusion for a few hours riding atop the green John Deere, looking across field and forest, feeling pleasantly alone yet connected to the land.

Boss gave me a pocketknife the first week of that summer. He said to keep it handy because a knife can make a lot of quick fixes on a farm. I still have that knife and wear it most days. Sometimes I use it around the house to slice an orange or to cut a box open.

I drove home sweaty and exhausted most days, using the commute to rehydrate and think. Ideas rolled around in my head as my navy blue Honda cruised on those dusty gravel roads and paved county highways. Working on the farm helped me sleep better at night and made me feel like I'd accomplished something real.

I learned how to work hard that summer, getting my hands dirty with earth and hay under the sun. I didn't easily abandon tasks; I learned how to finish them before the day was over. It felt better to finish something before driving home to wash up and eat dinner. Perhaps that's where my father got his strong Midwestern work ethic, and his father before him. Generations of men and women learned to put in a hard and honest day's labor under the hot Heartland sun. I imagined what it must have been like to live on the unsettled Minnesota prairies, before hoards of other pioneer families descended on the fertile soil with their covered wagons and bonnets and rifles.

I was grateful to be a modern cowboy, other paths of life available to me, unlike the families centuries ago who may have had no other options because of a dried-up life back east.

I worked on the farm only for that one summer, until I eagerly moved into a college dorm that fall to continue my education. I knew farm work was only meant to be a season for me, and I had more pursuits beyond the hayfields and fence lines.

My mind became the fertile soil in which ideas were planted and cultivated, and I quickly learned that hard work manifests in different forms, too. It was a transition that would change the course of my life.

25

Significant Work

*"Work is about a search for daily meaning as well
as daily bread...for a sort of life rather than a
Monday-through-Friday sort of dying."*

STUDS TERKEL

When I was six or seven years old, I attended a day camp. The group took a field trip to a local river park to explore the outdoors. At one point during the day, I was separated from the group and got lost down the trails between the trees. When I came to another picnic area, unrecognizable people stared at me with strangers' eyes, and I cried.

I don't think it was the fact that I felt danger that made me cry. It was deeper than that; I think it was because I felt lost, disconnected from the people I belonged to. I was separated from my tribe, the people who knew me and cared about me.

One of my greatest fears is the fear of being alone—not in a sense that I think I'll be an abandoned recluse, but an anxious notion that I won't be meaningfully connected to anyone or contribute anything meaningful to the world. Nihilist depression darkens my outlook when I imagine a life and work that goes nowhere and does nothing. I don't know where it came from, but it's haunting and complex, because I love solitude even as my heart craves connection.

Why We Work

Whether by choice or by necessity, a lot of us get lost in our work. Time is an offering, the almighty office desk an altar. We live in a culture that praises overtime and sacrificed relationships with family and friends. Society deems it socially acceptable to be a workaholic—even though it's doubtful we actually accomplish more by working longer[61]—but few of us remember that's how we get burnt out and spiral out of control under the pressure of it all. The tension of a results-driven culture tempts us to sacrifice a little more time, a little more health. Why do we recognize such little middle ground between lazy entitlement and obsessive workaholism?

Working hard and passionately is to be commended; however, work is only one piece of the puzzle. It's meant to carry something. Work is designed for significance beyond itself.

Conflict erupts within ourselves and with others when we try to make work into something it's not. Many recognize that work carries intrinsic value as well as dignity and an income.[62] It's not just about individual achievement, wealth, or living comfortably. It's a connection thing. Without connections, our work doesn't live up to its potential. Work is about purpose, and our purpose is connected to people.

There's a really depressing book in the Old Testament called Ecclesiastes. Its narrator self-identifies as "Teacher" and "king over Israel," yet draws sharp contrast against other wisdom literature in the ancient world and the lessons they taught—including the life and writings of Solomon.[63]

King Solomon was considered the wisest man in the world around 1000 BC. He was royalty, sitting on his throne in Israel—one of the most influential nations of that time. Nothing was withheld from him. Over time, he amassed wealth, military assets, and a thousand wives and mistresses.[64] With his many successes, it would seem that he should've been the happiest man in the world, with nothing but celebration and cheer for all his days.

Despite all he had, Solomon wasn't satisfied. The cultural measure of success didn't work for one of the world's most successful people. In critique of the conquering and accumulation mindset, the narrator of Ecclesiastes revealed what really mattered was much simpler than that:

> Again I saw something meaningless under the sun: There was a man all alone; he had neither son nor brother. There was no end to his toil, yet his eyes were not content with his wealth. "For whom am I toiling," he asked, "and why am I depriving myself of enjoyment?" This too is meaningless—a miserable business! Two are better than one, because they have a good return for their labor: if either of them falls down, one can help the other up. But pity anyone who falls and has no one to help them up. Also, if two lie down together, they will keep warm. But how can one keep warm alone? Though one may be overpowered, two can defend themselves. A cord of three strands is not quickly broken.[65]

What if we're looking in the wrong places to find a fulfilled life? How silly humanity's pursuits often are. Satisfaction isn't found by owning more things, controlling more people, or getting instant gratification. Working toward self-satisfaction is shortsighted; we're made for more than that.

Life is more than what we achieve. Our work isn't everything, but it isn't nothing.

I don't want to look back on my life with remorse because I hoped for fulfillment in the wrong things. Work is not just a means to an end, and I don't want to mistake that end for something it's not. Author John Mark Comer points out: "What you do for work matters just as much as, if not more than, what you do with the money you make from your work."[66]

Work is about providing for the people we love, and it's how we contribute to the world and make our mark in it. Work teaches us to grow and change, and it helps us discover parts of who we are, but it's not the only thing that defines us. The number of zeros on the end of our paycheck or upward trends on our performance reviews could never quantify the value of our existence.

The substance of our lives is found in the simpler things that call out for us daily, like knowing our role in the world and being a good friend, neighbor, and family member. We find our purpose by learning to become the person God's dreamed us to be, and by doing work that adds to human flourishing. Comer also wrote, "We can glorify God by doing our work in such a way that we make the invisible God visible by what we do and how we do it."[67]

We find the true meaning of work when we realize it's about striving for something eternally significant and connecting with people, not trying to gain something from them.

26

Group Showers

*"A good laugh and a long sleep are
the best cures in the doctor's book."*

IRISH PROVERB

Since we were old enough to drive, my high school friends and I had a summer ritual of going to a huge three-day music festival in central Minnesota. Dozens of Christian bands would perform on one of the five different stages, and a lot of the independent bands would try to gain some followers and sell merch at the smaller stages. For music fans like us, this was paradise.

The summer before my senior year of high school, we made the annual trek to the middle of the state's endless cornfields. As was tradition, we set up camp with a circle of tents near the tennis courts, lounged around with Pop Tarts and Mountain Dew for breakfast, and stayed up late with the sounds and lights of live performances washing over us. It was our own Woodstock, with the same kind of neighborliness, but with obscene amounts of sugar and tacky Christianese T-shirts instead of narcotics and free love.

Attendance for the festival hovered around 20,000 people. With such a massive invasion of the small farm town, the local high school allowed concertgoers to use their shower facilities to cool down and clean up. As a rather adamant introvert who never cared for the locker room environment, going to shower with dozens of strangers wasn't an inviting thought. Even more, I hated the idea of going three full days at outdoor concerts without cleaning off the layers of sweat and dust.

One day of the festival, I headed to the school for a refreshing shower. Like any other locker room in America, jests of male physique and boasts of machismo saturated the air like the humidity from hot showers. After setting down my clothes and towel, I made my way to the end of the long line of men, shampoo and soap in hand.

Perhaps because my mind was on other things, or maybe because I wished to clean off quickly and get back to the concerts, I failed to notice the lack of friction of the wet floor tiles.

Without warning, my feet slid out from under me, leaving me laid out on the soapy floor. The shampoo bottle and bar of soap flew out of my hands. My backside cushioned the fall, but not my ego. I bashfully stood back up and continued my shuffle to the back of the line, to the snickers of onlookers. It seemed like thirty more men were added to the queue, prolonging my walk of shame while I avoided eye contact with other festivalgoers.

Not a few paces further, in my embarrassed stupor, the soapy tile floor again caught me unaware. Up went the feet; away flew the shampoo and soap; further out of reach slid my self-confidence.

Some people can resist chuckling at a guy who trips over himself once in public, but no one can hold back a burst of cackling laughter when he slips twice and lands on his butt in a locker room with a hundred naked men in attendance.

When I finally made it to the front of the line, I couldn't wash up and get dressed fast enough. That must have been the shortest shower I had ever taken, and within minutes I returned to the group campsite and hid in my tent to let the moment dissolve behind me.

In the moment, it made me want to give up and never shower again—or, more specifically, never be in such an uncomfortable situation again.

It's inevitable we'll face moments of humiliation. "Shame corrodes the very part of us that believes we are capable of change."[68] Those moments can make or break us, if we let them. But with a good sense of humor, we'll find they can be memories that remind us we all lose our grip every once in a while. We can allow moments of failure to become shame or simply blips on the radar of the journey in which we're moving forward.

We choose what we allow to define us.

We can also choose when and under what circumstances we take showers.

MOVEMENT THREE

Refinement

27

When Love Isn't Sexy

"Those who invest themselves in becoming their best selves, and even more importantly, those who invest themselves in helping others become their best selves, are involved in the most important work possible on the face of the earth, they are helping to complete God's work."

ERIC HOFFER

There's nothing like testing the bonds of love when you're cooped up with your family for a long time.

When I was a teenager, my parents and siblings and I packed into a silver Dodge Caravan and took the interstate out of Minnesota. We'd visit relatives in Iowa and Florida, learn in the shadows of historical landmarks in Washington, D.C., or marvel at the wild expanse of Wyoming and Colorado.

Being stuffed into a minivan with four other people meant no two individuals wanted to pass time in the same way or listen to the same music. Though I inherited our mother's brown hair and brown eyes, we each had a will of our own. As was our custom, we plugged headphones into our own portable CD players. My older sister, Laura, read books and created scrapbooks to document our family adventures. My younger brother, Lee, and I fell captive to the worlds within our Game Boys and CD collections.

My mother occasionally listened to books on tape, probably because it reminded her of family vacations on the road during her childhood. My father often tuned the radio to a classical station and toggled the music only through the front driver-side speaker, which annoyed me to no end. I told him music was meant to be heard from two balanced speakers, as the human ears were so obviously positioned. He resisted my pristine logic, the edge of his mouth curling into a slight smirk to accompany a glance from his sharp blue eyes hidden behind thick glasses.

When I was old enough to drive, my parents wanted help during long travel days, so I took shifts at the steering wheel. I played punk and alternative CDs, using finger drumming on the steering wheel and air guitar strumming to stay focused on the road. Music wasn't just my transporting escapism; it became engaging art that made me even more aware of the moments that made up my life.

Dad often told me to turn down the aggressive music or restrict it to the front driver-side speaker, but I insisted it helped me focus on safe driving. Mom smiled knowingly from the middle row bucket seat, reminding Dad I was a trustworthy driver and that music was good for me.

That's one of the ways I know love is real and intensely practical, even if we have a hard time explaining what love is.

Defining Love

We've become familiar with love portrayed in films and novels, modern neuroscience explaining the chemical reactions that create romantic feelings, and ever-morphing social norms, but those don't necessarily tell us what love is supposed to be. They simply show us current explorations of it.

Is love always sexy and romantic? Is it that warm, fuzzy feeling accompanying a moment of intimacy? Is it the joys of family, like reuniting over Thanksgiving dinner or being together to open Christmas presents?

Is love the rigid determination to diminish ourselves so the people we care about can get their way? Parents may sense they must oblige their children's desires or risk losing their affection. Lovers tell each other what they think the other wants to hear so they can continue the relationship in which one or both may have become unhappily resigned long before.

Either of these makes love a formula, more concerned with fulfilling an expectation than connecting with a person. Yet there's another option, rich in both simplicity and complexity.

The most difficult and beautiful understanding of love is mutual self-giving. We often praise people as heroes if they completely deny themselves for others, yet even that falls short of the value that mutual, two-way sacrifice offers both parties. Love is hard work and requires patience and grace, even if it isn't sexy in the Hollywood sort of way. Out of an attitude of humility, people who love make space for the other to show up and be his or her best self. With patience, we learn to not always give our loved ones what they demand when they demand it, but to help them find the right thing at the right time. Love is gracious because it freely gives to another, but it doesn't diminish our worth when we uphold someone else's worth.

Real love benefits both the one giving it and the one receiving it. It's not only for romance and marriage, but for families and friendships, too. Love is an equalizing humility: it's not thinking less of yourself, but thinking of yourself less.

The way my parents were on those long car rides across the country is the kind of love that comes to mind when I consider self-sacrifice. It wasn't a very demanding version of sacrifice, but it reminds me of looking out for someone beyond myself. Sometimes love means letting go of our own preferences for a moment or a season. Other times, it may mean compassionately confronting the beloved with a harsh reality she hasn't yet realized, but allowing her the choice to change for the sake of her long-term health and growth.

The Truth About Love

When the spring weather breaches the 60s and the rainy clouds of winter evacuate Southern Oregon, I get outside and walk some trails.

One spring day of the third year I lived in Oregon, I struck out to hike a local peak with three friends. It's good for the soul to explore new territory with a few fellow adventurers. We left the trailhead as the sun grazed westward in the cloud-littered sky. Light peeked between some of the dark, western clouds like beacons warning of threatening weather not far behind us in the east.

When we reached the top and made our way over to a rocky lookout point, our conversation halted in favor of the beautiful view that begged for our attention. After a few moments of silence, gazing across the Rogue Valley from 2,000 feet up, the conversation turned to other topics.

A couple of the guys acknowledged the common frustration of seeing other friends struggling with some personal issues, making poor life choices, or walking away from God. People never seem to do what you want them to. Relationships are messy and risky because people are messy and complex. If imperfect people spend time with other imperfect people, there's a high probability—hovering around 100%—imperfections will surface. But where's the balance of loving other people and carefully calling out their imperfections that keep them from moving forward?

That question bothered me because it illuminated the conflict of what I felt I should do and what I thought I should do. Thoughts and feelings make a mess of things we already had sorted out, don't they? But then I remembered a story.

In the first century AD, a mentor named John wrote a letter to a group of Jesus' followers, urging them to remember an old commandment from God. The old commandment, which John redefined as new and relevant as ever, explained why we can't be right with God if we're holding out on loving the people around us:

> Anyone who claims to be in the light but hates a brother or sister is still in the darkness. Anyone who loves their brother and sister lives in the light, and there is nothing in them to make them stumble.[69]

In the darkness of our fragmented lives, we operate outside of connection with other people, without their help, without honest communication and healthy challenges for our growth. It's easy to live in darkness because it hides us; we don't have to admit we're wrong. But we're not meant to live in that darkness.

Throughout the Bible, God tells humanity he wants to invade our darkness, reveal our imperfections, and extract the sins that hinder us from living a whole, forgiven, and fulfilled life. The reason God calls out our sins isn't so he can be a cosmic killjoy; it's to remove things that get in the way of our health and flourishing. If we can really find the best joy in connection with him, God is gracious to remove those barriers that misplace our happiness in things that will ultimately disappoint us.[70] Our souls were made for so much more; Jesus came to rescue us from those lesser things.

When we look at our relationships, we can choose to see other people through the lens of God's love. His love goes a lot further and deeper than ours can. The point of Jesus' love is not about a feel-good sentiment or earning religious favoritism, but about a life-giving connection with him. Jesus sets the example so we see how to love someone: caring for people is about pointing them to better things and helping them get there.

Loving God is inextricably tied to loving people.[71] God's invitation to live in a relationship with him means that we're also connected to other people he is in a relationship with. Our connection with others looks different depending on things like proximity, trust, and seasons of life, but love allows those variations. It's a demanding challenge to love people who have as many imperfections as we do. But knowing Jesus is knowing our place in God's family—a family that loves each other. We cannot claim to belong to God's family if we do not love the people who belong to God.[72]

Deciding to Stay

On the mountain, my friend Bradley told us about one of his friends from college. He had noticed some pretty obvious ways in which his friend was acting dismissive and destructive, disregarding the health of a relationship and the God he claimed to follow. When Bradley confronted him about it, his friend passed it off as unimportant and irrelevant because he didn't see it the same way Bradley did. Bradley wanted to help his friend, a fellow Christian, return to a better way of life in connection with Jesus.

Bradley said something I had to think about for a moment: "At some point, I had to decide whether I wanted the self-satisfaction of being right or the opportunity to keep him as my friend."

In an uncomfortable situation, Bradley approached his friend and lovingly pointed him to something better—God's help recalibrating a relationship—but his friend declined. Instead of calling off the friendship, Bradley chose to remain his friend. Bradley didn't neglect the truth of the situation, but he continued to offer his friend love regardless of the choices he made.

Love doesn't always need to be acknowledged as right. That's a hard teaching I often resist because I like stating the reality of a matter, yet love takes care of that on its own. Truth and love are mysteriously intertwined, braided together to bring us clarity and belonging. Truth motivates love. When we know who God is and who he's made us to be, we can love at our fullest capacity. By extending that love to other people, we find that to love is to express the very presence of God.

28

Brotherhood

"A true friend sticks closer than a brother."
SOLOMON

When I was around 10 years old, my life consisted of watching *Star Wars*, building LEGOs, and playing outside. Those were the ingredients of my closest friendships, too.

My friend Sean knew that better than anyone. I looked up to him: he most closely resembled a Jedi in his knowledge of *Star Wars* and LEGO prowess. Plus he was significantly taller than me and later became the first of my classmates with legitimate facial hair to match his reddish-brown locks, which were styled like Luke Skywalker's.

What seemed like every other weekend, Sean and I begged one or the other's parents to permit a sleepover, which inevitably included adventures in a galaxy far, far away.

We had it down to a science: getting our fill of Super Nintendo, building new LEGO creations, and consuming frozen pizza with root beer while binge-watching *Star Wars*.

Sean didn't have a sibling to play with, or get into trouble with, or eat frozen pizzas with, except his much older brother who rarely visited from his home in Alaska or somewhere rugged. I could only be his friend, but hoped I could be a good one. I was eager to get away from my sister and brother, whom I considered bossy and annoying, respectively. Sean seemed eager for someone his age with similar interests. Through those *Star Wars* and LEGO weekends, we became not just friends, but also brothers.

A Friend for Every Adversity

My brother, Lee, once badly scraped his knees on a field trip. He's always been the athletic one, eyes wide with focus and a flash of arms and legs breezing past me on every field, road, and trail. The camp counselors called me to the bus seat where he lay. Lee remembers me offering my hand for him to squeeze because of the pain while a counselor plucked gravel from his sweaty skin and streams of crimson blood rolled down his legs. Moments like that tell me a brother's presence and affirmation carry unique significance. Other relationships certainly have their own power, yet brotherhood holds a strength of its own.

One writer of the Bible portrays it beautifully in a proverb: "A friend loves at all times, and a brother is born for a time of adversity."[73]

I can look back on years of meaningful events, lackluster romances, and wavering seasons, and all throughout them have been steadfast brothers by my side. Without the closest of friends, most of life's experiences would lose their richness. We're not meant to drift through life alone, but instead to live our stories anchored in relationships.

Years ago, I talked to a friend before he flew out of the country to start the next phase of his life. I didn't know when he'd return. I asked if he felt sad about leaving all the people he knew in the States. His reply was astonishing: "I've found that God provides the right friends to be around me for each different place in life."

Even if certain friendships don't continue through all of one's life, a person can be influenced largely by those temporary relationships. God provides the people we need around us during each chapter, to help us through conflicts, and for us to help them as well.

In each stage, in each place, I've had the friends I needed to challenge me, give me space for solitude, encourage me, and keep me moving forward. That's not to say friends never vanish.

Some days I wonder about the relationships that didn't make it because we lost touch, moved away, or something turned sour. Yet for a select few of those special brothers or sisters, there's untold reward in maintaining a relationship over time and distance despite the separation of where life has taken us.

C. S. Lewis once wrote, "To the Ancients, friendship seemed the happiest and most fully human of all loves; the crown of life, and the school of virtue."[74]

Sincere friendships have the power to enrich our lives, but also teach us more about the world. To identify so closely with a brother or sister enables us to learn what life is really like for someone else, without pretense or facade. When you call a friend your brother, you don't keep him at arm's length; you learn to share his perspective, fears, and hopes. A sister doesn't just know how you take your coffee; she knows which coffee shops you'll never revisit because it's where your ex-boyfriend used to work and you're still processing some of what happened. Intimacy is the core of deep friendships; it's when you say to a trusted companion, *This is something I've never told anyone else, but I trust you with my secrets.*

Keeping a friend who sticks closer than a brother or sister becomes difficult, whether from a conflict in your personalities, a conversational pain point, or the natural erosion of good intentions to stay connected. But if we step back and look at the endless variables of where we've lived, what we've done, and who we've connected with, we realize the friendships that impact us the most weren't just about our intentions in the first place: "The friendship is not a reward for our discrimination and good taste in finding one another out. It is the instrument by which God reveals to each the beauties of all the others."[75]

Perhaps God orchestrates the relationships we can choose because he knows what—and who—we need in each chapter of our lives.

29

Not Easily Surrendered

"The only way to have a friend is to be one."
RALPH WALDO EMERSON

It was fall in Greenville, South Carolina—a city that would provide the setting for more important moments of my story than I ever anticipated. In October of the year I moved to Oregon, four of us sat around a hotel room in the heart of the charming Southern downtown. It was late, after a full day attending the conference of an organization we had done volunteer work with.

Each of us lived in different cities around the country, so I was eager to catch up with them. Brian was directing media and communications for a church in Eastern Washington. The brothers, Seth and Nate, were in Minneapolis. Seth had just been hired for a job based there, which included a regular dose of travel. Nate was leading the church on the University of Minnesota campus, and he'd recently started talking with a girl from Utah he'd met a couple months earlier. (He was smitten, and we were not surprised when he proposed to Robyn before the year was out.) I was six months into my job in Oregon, and I sorely missed the nearness of my friends.

The lights of the Greenville horizon shone between tree branches up and down the streets, just outside our hotel room window. Nearing midnight and feeling the gravity of sleepiness, our conversation slowed but our hearts still resonated with a bond like brothers who'd grown up together, companions and competitors alike.

We certainly had our share of scuffles—they're impossible to avoid when you're college roommates, when assumptions and expectations prove your selfish ignorance of each other, and when some minds change about a topic while others don't. Though separated after several years of important lessons and enduring challenges together, after frustrating fights and working side by side to resolve them, something stirred within us to continue that growth. We didn't want our friendships to fizzle out, lackluster and stale.

As I reflected on that night, I became grateful for their companionship. We had to figure out a way to stay connected across the miles. It would not be easy, but it would be worthwhile. Later, I hacked away on my computer to produce what would be a new entry on my blog, attempting to process the relational and spiritual significance of the night.

Blog Post: A wild weekend, but not the kind you'd think.

Sometimes certain thoughts are clearer and more distinct and make more sense—without making complete sense—than the others that surround them. I need to be intentional about the relationships and opportunities I already have.

Changes are on the horizon. Refocusing is in order. Refining of priorities and time spent and passions instilled and connections made. I'm not sure of all the details—hardly any, in fact.

A large part of this lies in the huge blessing of being in the same room with my three best and closest friends. This has not happened in a full year. Substantial, yet a continuation of what has already been brew-

ing: refocusing of life vision, direction, passions, and giftings and perhaps, just maybe, a reorientation of divine calling.

Another evidence of the expansive kingdom of God. He does big stuff. Way too big for us to orchestrate. We can hardly even keep up.

If our lives were a movie, this was a major plot point, a moment of change. Our friendships fought the battles of distance and apathy, but resolved not to give in to the conflict. We were moving forward.

The next morning, Nate wrote a blog post, too. The moment seemed far bigger than the four of us.

Nate's Blog Post: In a room with three major players in my life last night.

I sat in a room with three other men: John, Brian, and Seth. We have shared more of life together in the past seven years than some will share in their lifetime.

We now live far away from one another, but these types of friendships are the lifelong friendships. The type of friendship where you could not talk in two months, or see each other in a year, and still pick up where you left off. How does something stand the test of time, stand the test of distance, and still stand stronger than some relationships where people live in the same city?

Seven years ago, my dad listened to the call of God on his life, and at the beginning of that summer, our family moved from Southwest Iowa to Rochester, Minnesota. My dad always said, "I don't believe God just calls me, but God calls the family."

Because of my dad's obedience, I ended up in Min-

nesota. One of the hardest times of my life, but in hindsight, the best thing that ever happened to me.

Because of my dad's obedience, and my family's obedience, my brother met Brian soon after he started school. Brian knew John. They played music. Seth told me I needed to meet them. I met them a few weeks later.

But who in the world could've guessed seven years ago what the future held for us...

"For my thoughts are not your thoughts, neither are your ways my ways," declares the Lord. "As the heavens are higher than the earth, so are my ways higher than your ways and my thoughts than your thoughts." [76]

Seth and I grew closer than we ever would have if my family had not moved. I have held few men as I have held these three, in tears. They know a thing or two about "just being there" when a friend is hurting, and not saying something dumb when no words will help the situation. We have visited very dark places and very good places in life together.

This weekend is the first time in a year the four of us have been in the same room. Somehow, God is the growth, reason, and sustainer of these deep relationships that should have dissolved when distance came into the picture, or when it had been a few months since we last talked. When I think of these men, I echo the prayer of Paul as he wrote to the Philippians:

I thank my God every time I remember you.

In all my prayers for all of you, I always pray with joy because of your partnership in the gospel from the first day until now, being confident of this, that he who began a good work in you will carry it on to comple-

tion until the day of Christ Jesus. It is right
for me to feel this way about all of you,
since I have you in my heart...[77]
God has started something and he is at work to
complete it. He delights to give his children good gifts.
How blessed we are.

Friends of the Heart

It's been said there are two kinds of friendship: friendship of the road and friendship of the heart. Friendship of the road carries on as long as both people travel in the same direction on the journey of life, but a time comes when their paths diverge. Friendship of the heart goes deeper than a shared path because identities connect to form a unique bond.

Having a close friend by your side multiplies your confidence and reinforces your faith. Close friends don't just bloom because they've known each other for years. Some people know each other a lifetime but never gain deep friendship. Shared hobbies can't always sustain best friends because hobbies come and go. We know sheer volume of time spent together doesn't necessarily breed friendship: although we spend the most consistent time around coworkers and immediate family, most of us have deep friendships outside of those categories.

Friendship is a crop planted by God and cultivated by our intentionality. Deep friendship is built on purpose, over time, with trust, and through shared experiences. Despite the challenges of time and distance, we remain committed to each other. We've got each other's backs when one of us faces conflict, and we share in rejoicing with each other's successes. "To always be here for you; that is true friendship."[78]

Genuine friends don't just share conversations; they play an active role in each other's stories. A friendship of the heart is not easily surrendered.

I hope you've experienced this kind of friendship. I expect I'll have several more over the course of my life, for each stage of life needs close relationships. Throughout your life, I hope you give and receive the support required to live a meaningful story.

30

Game Boys and the Abundant Life

*"The choice we face (in life) is between empty
self-indulgence and meaningful activity."*

BILLY GRAHAM

If you grew up when I did, you remember the bright glow of video game screens on the foreheads of our generation.

All my middle school friends had game systems hooked up to TVs in their bedrooms. They even had handheld Game Boys so they could go through a whole day, school or not, without ever being separated from their gaming. Those little flashing screens were like cocaine, but kids don't think about that kind of thing, how addictions keep us from living the life in front of us.

Lee and I begged our parents for Game Boys. We had already exhausted our interest of computer games, which felt too limited and clunky. Minimizing sedentary time had long been a Weirick family principle, so TV viewing was limited to an hour per day. Lee and I surpassed that immediately after school while we shoveled cereal into our mouths from large mixing bowls.

For our birthdays one year, my parents gave us each a Game Boy. We sat on the couch playing as much as Mom would let us, and she had to pry our eyes away from the tiny screens when she called us to set the dinner table. I lay in bed those nights trying to fall asleep but replaying game levels in my mind.

Having my own video games seemed too good to be true. Before I actually owned any, I felt I was missing out on a big event in my childhood and falling out of the graces of my friends. Young boys and girls can be fickle. Sometimes we don't grow out of it.

The Materialism Cycle

It's the same way with a lot of human desires. We latch on to the idea of something new and shiny and better, and we judge our success in life by how close we are to that object of desire. Everything becomes about getting it, about fulfilling the craving.

As a child, it manifested as an obsession with a video game I didn't have. And like all things, once I had gotten it, the newness wore off. After a few weeks or months, the little old Game Boy wasn't good enough, but I thought the new and improved version would be. And then the bigger, newer one, and then the big TV console system.

For adults in a productivity- and success-driven world, materialism is the acceptable, modern idol of choice. It's a vice that usually isn't called a vice. Like jonesing for a fix, the materialist in you and me pangs for just a little bit more. *One more car. Upgrade the computer and smartphone. Perhaps there will be room in this year's budget to allow for the summer home we've always wanted. Just a few more shopping sprees. Those shoes were such a great deal, and so are those, and those; how could I pass them up?*

I know—some days, that's where my thoughts go, too.

There's a vicious cycle of poverty, but I also think there's a cycle of materialistic wealth that's just as brutal. It's dangerous the way we slide into the rut of accumulation.

Materialism says the goal of life is to gain. There's even a popular bumper sticker that says, "He who dies with the most toys wins."[79] When we subscribe to this mentality, we worship at the altar of our whims and the marketplace. People are only seen as assistance or hindrance in the pursuit of accumulating more things. We abandon character because it's inconvenient to live with integrity when more things can be acquired dishonorably.

I'm not saying it's wrong to work to get more things. Working hard to earn a living and provide for people we love is a noble and worthy pursuit. God wants us to figure out our lives and what work we'll pour our energy and passion into. But God urges us to value him and the people around us more than we value wealth or pursuit of it. One rabbi wrote, "There is happiness in the love of labor, there is misery in the love of gain."[80]

Abundance

There's a story in the Bible in which Jesus explained what it's like to know God.[81] Since his listeners were in a first-century rural agricultural setting, Jesus portrayed his relationship to people like a shepherd leading and caring for sheep.

During cool evenings in ancient Israel, shepherds kept their flocks safe in fenced sheepfolds to fend off wild animals and keep the sheep from straying. Shepherds slept at the gate of the fold so that whatever tried to attack or steal the sheep had to pass by the protective shepherd first.

A shepherd had no need of sneaking into the sheepfold because he already had access to the sheep through the gate. So someone who jumped the fence to gain access to the sheep was suspect. Thieves jump fences. Wolves jump fences. Shepherds enter through the gate—or in a way, they became the gate.

Jesus called himself the good shepherd, one who looked out for the safety and wellbeing of his sheep, his people. He said, "The thief does not come except to steal, and to kill, and to destroy. I have come that they may have life, and that they may have it more abundantly."[82]

When our lives become more about gaining, we move further away from the kind of life Jesus was talking about. People who seek to accumulate more will run into the hard reality that accumulation doesn't equal unlimited satisfaction. Abundance in material things doesn't equal abundant life.

Abundant life is found in knowing God and shaping our lives around him. Wholeness isn't found in getting or taking, achieving or actualizing, or even in acting charitably. We are designed for a relationship with God, understanding who he is and who we are in relation to him. He intends good for us, and to do good through us, because he cares deeply about each member of the human race, little bearers of his image.

I'm grateful God doesn't manipulate us and take things from us with mean-spirited intentions. He's no thief. He's so far away from thievery that he gave us himself. We are given Jesus, the shepherd of our souls, the one who leads us into fresh pastures and a new way of living. We are given his Spirit, a guide and advocate, a gift to our soul's thirst for a life that matters.[83]

My new job in Oregon felt like fresh pastures, yet learning that abundance was less about possessions made me rethink my career a number of times. I couldn't let myself live to work to gain; it had to be more than that.

When we're exploring the new life God offers, our desires are transformed, too. We stop hoping in belongings to satisfy us. We're no longer content to spend our days scheming about additional things we can gain. Rather, learning to follow Jesus turns our greed into generosity. We leave a perspective of selfishness for a life of becoming healthy and helping others get healthy on the path to wholeness.

31

When God Speaks

*"Every moment and every event of every man's
life on earth plants something in his soul."*

THOMAS MERTON

One of the best jobs I ever had was traveling during the
summers between my college semesters. It was for a series
of weeklong mission trips held in twenty cities around North
America each year, and it became a ritual road trip I anticipated every summer.

The organization that ran those trips had it down to a science.
Four or five college students were on a team, and we packed
into a Ford Expedition and hauled a sixteen-foot trailer full of
sound equipment, office supplies, and lots of T-shirts to each
city. For two months, we drove to five or six locations around
the country, staying in one place for only a week at a time.

We lived out of suitcases, seeing new landscapes every seven
days, and I loved every minute of it (except for the lack of sleep
and solitude). It was my induction into the world of perpetual motion. The scenery was amazing, inspiring, and fresh to a
Midwestern boy who was constantly learning that the world
was even more vast and beautiful than he thought he knew.

I almost didn't go.

It takes decisive willingness to risk months at a time with
strangers and strange places away from the consistency of life

back home. I had never traveled like that before, for so long and with people I barely even knew. These variables looked more like conflict I wanted to avoid. It was my own crossing of the Rubicon: my timid, adamant introvert self shied away from the rushing waters of this new environment, but my yearning for adventure called out like a voice beckoning from the opposite riverbank.

There is something romantic about traveling distances, seeing things that one has never taken in before. Magnetic inclination draws us toward unknown things beyond the boundaries of our personal, known world. There are lands, cultures, and ideas one wouldn't normally consider if he stayed in the shelter of comfort people tend to live in. It's not romantic in a falling-in-love-with-someone sort of way, but is perhaps even deeper—a sense many of us acquire when the opportunity arises to explore and discover.

While traveling that summer, I inhaled the oxygen of possibility. I was firing on all cylinders—as one writer put it, "Travel makes the world look new, and when the world looks new, our brains work harder."[84] I was in love with the open road, drunk on the adventure of newness, and that intoxication would never be easily quenched again.

My first summer on staff, one of my teammates was from New Zealand. He looked like any other North American at first glance: curly blond hair, black-rimmed glasses, Chaco sandals, and screen T-shirts—but he spoke with a thoroughly Kiwi accent. He was rather reserved when I first met him, but it wasn't long before we were exchanging favorite music and quirky jokes. By the end of that summer, we had thrown around a Frisbee in nearly every one of the twenty-some states we'd visited. The best place was across the U.S.-Canada border near Vancouver, despite the unimpressed border agents. The worst was near the horsefly-infested bogs of Louisiana, just over the East Texas border. We decided we did not care for Louisiana.

New Encounters

The summer mission projects were designed to introduce students to how churches started. High schoolers and chaperones listened to speakers and partnered with church planters to serve in communities around the city, making connections and doing good because God cared about the people there.

It's a beautiful thing to see young people awaken to a new reality, to engage an idea and not be afraid of getting their hands dirty in the process. A lot of the students I met during those summers impacted me because of the way they were willing to go all in with this God they were beginning to encounter in a fresh, new way.

I jumped at the chance when they offered me a leadership role for a weeklong project in Atlanta. After a while of calling Oregon home, I was grateful for an opportunity to revisit the organization and their work. I flew to Georgia to meet the summer staff team before the nine student groups arrived in the South's face-melting humidity. It was an exciting and enjoyable week. The students were enthusiastic, sharing how they were learning to see the church as people rather than a building, and putting faith into action.

Halfway through the week, our team planned something special. That evening, 120 high school students and leaders huddled together in groups under the auditorium's dim lights. The concert of prayer was a worship gathering with the purpose of helping students listen to, talk with, and express gratitude to God. With calm, ambient music playing in the background, we prompted students to pray for specific things and told stories of how God changed lives through spiritual revivals and activism throughout history.

I prayed silently, thanking God for how he'd changed me, trying to discern what was in store for the next stage of my life: *God, I'm with you. I want to follow you closely. I am with you and how you're changing lives here this week, and I want to keep moving forward with you.*

I'm not one to say I've heard God's audible voice, that he spoke something specifically to me, or that he gave me some prophetic insight—for most of my life, I've never said that. But I think, in that moment, it was him: *No, I've been with you. And I've been with you for a long time.*

I almost burst into tears on the spot. I got that feeling in my gut—the nerve-wracking instinct you get when looking down from tall buildings, like a rush of fight-or-flight adrenaline. I had learned about God for years and heard that he still communicates with people, yet I had only just begun to hear him speak.

Learning to Listen

The more I thought about it, the more I became convinced that this wasn't the first time God spoke to me; it was simply the most profound experience I remember.

Now I think God speaks to me all the time. I sense him through the sunrise some mornings I get up early enough to see rays of light pierce the fog. In stillness, he says, *It's okay to rest a little while. I'll provide what you need.* He speaks affirmation in the moments I feel weakest, when I'm about to give up on someone else or on myself, when I'd rather hide at home with an endless Netflix queue: *You made a poor decision and you chose anger over healing, but I'll help you out of it.* More recently, I've seen God communicate peace and kindness in ways that seem absurd and illogical in the midst of argumentative, reactive politics, and he says to me, *I'm not done bringing good in the world. Faith will always be more powerful than fear.* And it makes me believe even when circumstances around me don't reflect that now, they will later.

I know that makes me sound like a crazy person, and I probably am a little bit. I also know it's the character of God to be with people wherever they are, and it's just like him to send messages in the moments we need them most.

God speaks all the time. It's not necessarily speaking in an audible voice or hearing something in the wind. He's constantly sending messages of life into people and calling us to bigger things. The tension lies in knowing that he communicates and actually hearing what he says. If only we could listen closely, put down the smartphone and turn off the television, we might hear God clearly—if only for a moment.

Nowadays, I try to create space in my schedule to simply sit and listen, to turn off the car stereo for a commute or to stare out a window in silence. I love hiking in solitude, wondering what God will teach me next and how long it will be until he sends me on another cross-country road trip. He tells me I have no idea how different the next adventure will be.

I've asked him a lot of questions because I am curious and secretly insecure that my life won't amount to anything. Often, I ask for more adventures and deeper knowledge. Sometimes God is silent, like a friend who nods in understanding when there is nothing else to say for now. But he usually gives me the impression that he's got something good in store and things will be okay. An unexpected conversation with a friend's cheerful voice and stunning acts of love from someone close help me hear the heartbeat of the divine, right in the middle of the ordinary. And in the meantime, he reminds me, he knows the challenges I'm facing and hears my complaints. He knows because he is with me and he has been for a long time.

God is present in our stories, and we're better for it when we make space to listen for what he might say.

32

What We Can't Have

"When we are no longer able to change a situation,
we are challenged to change ourselves."

VIKTOR FRANKL

Brian says it's ironic that during college we thought our lives would be easier to manage after graduation. We anticipated with bated breath the moment when our lives would emerge from the cocoon of a rigidly scheduled formal education to spread wide our wings of academic freedom and seemingly endless potential. What now? The path is vast before us, any which way to go. We think we've regained control of our time and our responsibilities that seemed so bulky in our school years. We've arrived at what we've assumed will be a manageable existence.

Yet the weeks and months go by, post-graduation life ramping up to an unknown summit we think is so close. But what if it's actually decades or more removed from where we look? What if we're only out of the starting block instead of nearing the finish line?

This same feeling shows up in a variety of ways throughout our variable lives: we want what we can't have. It's a perpetual conflict between our expectations and our reality; another place and status is more desirable than the one in which we currently reside. We think to ourselves: *Will graduation solve*

my problem? Will an incredible job or a perfect someone give me
the feeling of completion? When will my family reach a place of
stability or success? When will I arrive?

We chase that elusive satisfaction, grasping for meaning
in daily drudgery. We feel relief if we simply make it through
the day.

There will always be a void to fill. There will always be an
unavoidable magnetism to whatever's out of reach. The grass is
always greener on the other side of the fence, we're told.

Dealing with Chaos

Though it's not a pleasant reality to admit, we can never have
full control of our existence. We're not meant to. Life is messy,
and the universe is littered with chaos.

Chaos bothers me. I like cleanliness and organization. That's
probably anchored in the subconscious structure of my youth,
the rigid rule-keeping and aversion to ambiguity in all things
spiritual and practical. Yet contrary to that magnetic attraction
to flawless order, I can't have it most of the time.

The chaos sternly requires me to surrender my desire for
control. I can't balance everything perfectly in the way I want
to, no matter how hard I try. Changing my life through will-
power is an appealing concept, but relentless disorder disman-
tles my efforts like wave after wave against a flood barrier in a
hurricane.

I cannot control the external world, but I can choose inner
resilience. It may not be calm in my circumstances, but I can
remain calm in my spirit.

Some seasons—I'm sure you've experienced this, too—I've
had to be consistent in small things and endure in what's less
than ideal, with the hope that someday, these circumstances
will be okay, adequate, what I've worked and waited for.

We don't have the slightest clue what our lives will look like a decade down the road, probably not even the five-year plan. I don't even know what the next month looks like, but knowing isn't the point. The appealing, ever-elusive next stage may need to stay on hold while I tune my eyes and mind to the beauty of my current status. God knows it's hard most of the time.

If we're drawn to the next step—if we desire what it holds for us as an escape from the present—maybe then we must remain in the current one for just a little longer. That's where we learn from the discomfort. That's not an excuse to sit back and do nothing. The key is acting with the agency of choices we can make in the midst of our present situation.

Contentment and hope are simultaneous catalysts for our growth. When chaos surrounds us, contentment anchors us. It's through discomfort that we grow the most. Faced with conflict from within ourselves or from outside forces, we're compelled to accept what we cannot control, but adjust our attitudes. When we accept that something is out of our control, we can focus on making the best choices about things within our control.

God has given us a map of possibilities and we're invited to chart the course of our lives with the decisions we make. We venture across the oceans of different worldviews and plant ourselves in relationships for times short or long. We seek new horizons of experience and, in the process, learn to enjoy the world as it is. We also dream of what it could be, what we can build into our plot as a contribution to the whole.

There's a magnet on the refrigerator at my in-laws' house that reads, "We cannot direct the winds but we can adjust our sails."[85] That is a sermon for all of us.

We cannot control the winds and waves on unrelenting seas. We cannot perfectly predict or manipulate the weather we're subjected to. But we can choose how we experience, process, and respond to what happens to us. The best way to manage our variable lives is to remember ultimate control belongs to none of us. It's the kind of humility we need to embrace the changes while letting go of the control we think we need.

Maybe it's better when we let go of what we can't control, adjust what we can, and learn to enjoy the ride.

33

Basketball

*"Practice is the hardest part of learning, and
training is the essence of transformation."*

ANN VOSKAMP

Basketball was a big deal when I was a teenager.

Lee and I shot hoops in our neighbor's backyard half-court nearly every evening of summer. We asked my parents to help us buy a Michael Jordan jersey and a Scotty Pippin jersey to wear while we played. Of course, I believed myself to be Jordan, though Lee was the far more athletic one. I was taller than him, but he was always faster. We didn't care to find our own Dennis Rodman.

I did a lot of thinking on those concrete slabs, where the world was simple. I imagined the surrounding trees to be crowds of fans cheering on my turnaround jump shot. The nearby pines loomed in anticipation of each free throw. Surely my basketball skills would impress the girls (but you can guess how that turned out).

Trying Out

When I was in seventh grade, my parents encouraged me to try out for the basketball team at our small private school. When I say I "tried out" for the school's basketball team, I mean that I told the coaches about my interest and showed up one Tuesday to practice. It wasn't a terribly official ordeal, but as a rather adamant introvert, I liked it that way. I knew they were desperate for more players on the junior high team because they still let me wear windbreaker pants during games. (Yes, it was cringe-worthy. No, I hadn't yet been peer-pressured into wearing sleek navy jersey shorts like everyone else.) Maybe I was psychologically grasping for something that felt like armor against a different environment, strangers, and unpredictable events in heavily air-conditioned gyms. "It is a sign of great inner insecurity to be hostile to the unfamiliar."[86] I couldn't hide forever in the safety of familiarity, away from the conflict of new experiences.

Over that winter, I rode the bench like it was made for me. On a few occasions, when our team had built a convincing 30-point lead over another unassuming, pitiful Christian school team, Coach would put me in with a few other scrawny second-stringers to get experience.

It felt good, playing basketball with a real audience. I even grabbed some rebounds and an assist. I imagined that was the same glimmer of expectation Jordan must've sensed when he played his first games as a kid. I was proud to wear the number 23 on my navy-and-white reversible jersey. *This is the start of my explosive athletic career*, I told myself.

Toward the end of the season, one of our away games looked to be an easy triumph because the other school had only middle school players. Coach thought it would be too harsh for us to play our starting lineup of high school giants. During warm-ups, he pulled me aside and asked me to be the starting power forward. I replied with a hesitant yes, and spent the next fifteen minutes eying our opponents across the court between rebounds and lay-up drills.

I had never started before. My basketball career was taking off.

City League

By the time the next fall came around, I was ready.

Being in eighth grade, I found that confidence came a little more naturally because I was older than most other middle school kids. Instead of playing with my school another season, I tried out for the city league with a couple of my school friends. We were put on the same team, practiced relentlessly at recess, and planned plays during Literature and Algebra, much to our classical Christian educators' dismay.

When it came time for picking jersey numbers, I once again snagged number 23. It had to be a good omen for my athletic career. I felt like magic with my black-and-gold jersey, black jersey shorts (I'd finally converted), and metallic Nike shoes.

The most memorable moment of my basketball career was during a game some of my older friends attended. A couple high school guys I looked up to in my church's youth group decided to watch me play one Saturday. The pressure was on. I felt the need to play even harder. These guys were starters on their high school teams, so they knew talent when they saw it. I hoped they'd see some in me.

Basketball was dangerous because pushy opponents nudged me closer to the precipice of anger, even though restraint was expected. I was assigned to cover a particularly tall, husky forward who had spiky blond hair and a dull stare, like a weary boxer who didn't know when to call it a day. He'd been giving me trouble the whole game because of his height advantage and aggressive pushes down by the basket. I knew I couldn't go ballistic on Husky Boy; our coach considered fouls inexcusable. As my team hustled back to set up defense, Husky Boy accepted a pass en route to the hoop. In a moment of brilliant clarity, I stepped into his path, planted my feet, and braced for impact.

It felt like slow motion. I hit the hardwood with a thud, laid out just in front of my older friends. They grinned with approval. Fans and parents erupted with cheering from the sidelines. Husky Boy unleashed on the referees—who dared call offensive charging on him—before he glared at me, the victim of his athletic crime.

I didn't pay Husky Boy much attention anymore. The gymnasium echoed with claps and shouts. They cheered for me. I tasted glory. It never felt so good to be knocked to the floor.

Tragedy or Trajectory

Memories like those often stand out more than events that mattered far more in my early years. Maybe you've got stories like that, too—stories you go back to in times of joy, nostalgia, discontent, or weakness. We all try to use the narrative of our history to define our present.

We keep chasing those same feelings even if they're remnants of the past. Those tastes of glory keep us going back to the same sources of affirmation, or the memories of pain keep us locked up and guarded against people who remind us of someone who hurt us earlier in life.

When we operate out of those emotions, we lose touch with our present ones. We trade the past we cannot change for the present we can, but we end up losing out on both if we don't snap back to reality. Author Ben Arment summed it up like this: "You can view the bad things in your life as either tragedy or trajectory."[87]

I'd like to say I'm good at remembering the moments that really mattered in my life, though it's a daily mind game. It's easy to inflate the importance of times that made me feel like a winner; it's more useful for my future if I understand experiences as the ingredients that formed the person I am today.

Good times and bad times alike, your story means something. It's not just a string of inconsequential events, but a series of moments and choices that give form to the mark you leave in the world. As long as you're still breathing and choosing, you can craft what your story looks like.

Even if you feel stuck in an old, repeating narrative, your story isn't over. You can keep pursuing experiences and doing things that matter. You can still savor the memory of a basketball game or cherish the perseverance that got you through the most painful conflict. And you can use the life behind you to clarify the kind of life you want before you.

34

God on the Whiteboard

*"Faith never knows where it is being led, but it
loves and knows the one who is leading."*

OSWALD CHAMBERS

One of the first awkward conversations I had when I moved to
Oregon was with Christian. I mistook him for a musician, so I
started asking him music questions until he pointed to someone else. It happened at the young adult community at Nick's
house, where a dozen of us would stay up late in awkward but
honest conversations. A few weeks in, I knew Christian and I
could be friends.

He was several years younger, built like a lean athlete, and he
could grow better facial hair than me. Christian was the kind of
friend who wasn't afraid to ask uncomfortable questions and
do crazy stunts, while still keeping his responsibilities in school
and work. He reminded me of my college years, when I met
so many different students who wanted to have fun and know
more about the world, neither at the expense of the other.

Two years after I moved to Oregon, I rented a house with
a couple guys, including Christian. We hung a whiteboard on
the kitchen wall and wrote a bunch of quotes on it. Over a few
months, it accrued a variety of sayings we'd heard from our role
models or lines from movies.

Christian had been dissecting an oyster of opportunity for

several months, hoping to find a pearl—a situation in which he could live affordably, continue with school and work, and help his family. He had options, but he was torn. News arrived that his family planned to move south to run a restaurant in Southern California. He had become one of my closest friends, so I could sense his internal wrestling match. It was the same kind of conflict that tore me between staying in Minnesota and leaving: one choice would change everything.

As an involved leader in the church's student ministry and young adult community, 19-year-old Christian offered the vibrancy of youthful energy and unbridled passion. He'd completed some college courses and, more importantly, discovered a God-given desire to be a pastor and teacher.

The first couple years I knew him, I saw Christian chasing this passion by volunteering lots of time to mentor middle school boys and preach messages for the students on Sunday mornings. He wasn't sure of all the details, but he knew the seed God planted in his soul. He cultivated it by honing his strengths and exorcising his weaknesses.

One April day, Christian wrote something new on the whiteboard. It was formed like poetry, with separate lines in black dry-erase marker:

> *It is time to move.*
> *I will no longer hold you where you are.*
> *It is spring and you are ready to be pushed forward.*
> *I will guide you and keep you.*
> *—God*

Christian had been building up the kind of life God led him into, but he still kept listening for his voice. There are times when we think we've got our lives nailed down, but God still has to give us a few course corrections to keep us on the path. Christian was doing what he already knew to do; then he stood attentive and ready as God prepared the next step for him. He worked while he waited.

Figuring out God's will is less about having answers and more about living with expectant hope. We can faithfully continue what we're presently in and keep looking forward. That kind of hope starts far away and seems almost impossible—like a distant plane in the night sky, giving away its location as wingtip lights reveal paths across the stars. The faint blinking lights are barely visible at times, but you can trace the path across the sky by remembering where it's been and connecting the dots to where it is.

Steve Jobs once told graduates at Stanford, "You can't connect the dots looking forward; you can only connect them looking backwards. So you have to trust that the dots will somehow connect in your future."[88]

God is connecting the dots for us all the time.

35

How to Be Refreshed

"Slow down and enjoy life. It's not only the scenery you miss by going too fast—you also miss the sense of where you are going and why."

EDDIE CANTOR

Kati and I dated for a year and then some. She finished a nursing degree while I learned how to persevere. The job that brought me to Oregon felt more like a burden than a blessing. *A job's a job,* I kept telling myself, trying to stay distracted with the friends I had grown close to and the woman I was learning to love.

I proposed near the trailhead of one of our favorite hikes, overlooking the valley on a sunny spring day. Her wavy, dark brown hair whipped in the wind as I kneeled and asked the question that would irreversibly change our lives. I had a pretty good idea of which response she would offer, but my insides shook nonetheless. She said yes—without too much hesitation, thankfully—while our friend Zak secretly snapped photographs from a car nearby. We were excited for the future, yet nervous about the details before us.

Oh, the details.

If you've ever been engaged to be married, you know it's like purgatory. It's the tension of waiting and planning and more waiting for an acknowledgement of the things you've already resolved in your heart and mind.

During the months leading up to our wedding, Kati and I grew increasingly stressed by the endless stream of details. We wanted the big day to be a grand event. After all, there were scores of friends, close family, and distant great aunts to impress. We saw it as an opportunity not just to focus on the start of our marriage, but also to celebrate the goodness of family and friends and the valuable roles they played in helping us become who we are.

The pressure was on. With the date growing ever closer, minimal frustrations bled into weary demeanor. Kati is made of tough stuff and I tend to tackle tasks head-on once I've wrestled internally for a bit, so we never doubted each other's ability to make things happen. We shared the load of preparations, as to each contribute to what was inherently supposed to be about loving and serving each other.

A month before our wedding date, we were noticeably fatigued. Kati was going through months of orientation for her new job at the hospital. Several consecutive weeks of stressful situations at work and demanding patients tested her endurance. I was working a job I didn't care for, frustrated in the work I was given and limited on what I could change within it. It didn't help that our food caterer for the wedding reception had neglected to return phone calls and e-mails for weeks. We tallied up costs. Our engagement photos were yet to be printed. Many RSVPs had yet to be returned. We pressed on, but the pile of tasks didn't seem to be getting smaller.

It saddened us to see each other's weariness grow more pronounced. I was at a loss for the right words or the right actions. How could I remedy the situation for her? How could she help me? Helplessness frustrated me. I like to fix problems; I wanted to solve these mentally distracting conflicts and relieve her of the stressors of the process. Kati readily admitted that, although she was committed to making the wedding a big celebration, part of her wished the whole ordeal would just be done and over with. It felt staggering, the constant attention required to stay on top of planning for the occasion.

See? Engagement is purgatory. It's an exasperating delay of the inevitable.

Avoiding an Agenda

In search of respite from the frantic wedding planning, one Saturday we drove down the interstate to Ashland, the most unique town in Southern Oregon.

Ashland always provides a revitalizing retreat. Unlike nearby cities' box store demeanors, eclectic Ashland is nestled close in the shadow of the Cascade Mountains. The town is a sort of combination of Portland, a Midwestern college town, and a Californian retiree village, with outgoing homeless citizens, wild and carefree college students, and Shakespeare-quoting vegans. The town is home to the Oregon Shakespeare Festival, and it prides itself in maintaining a quaint, eco-friendly, buy-local, artsy, cultural-center vibe. And it's quite charming; it quickly became one of my favorite places in the area.

Kati and I parked downtown, next to the Lithia Springs water fountains and drum circle. Before heading into the park, we stopped by one of our favorite spots, Noble Coffee, to pick up bold iced brews—chocolaty and tart, but never bitter.

Lithia Park is a series of walking paths, fertile gardens, duck ponds, playgrounds, and wooded groves, woven southward to the mountain. Passing noisy children on swing sets and families unfolding picnic spreads in the first few lawns, we found a quieter space back near the open-air band shell used by summer events.

For two hours, we rested in the shade of seventy-foot trees and a soothing breeze. The cheery voices of children flitted through the woods, joining with inquisitive birds chirping and an occasional leaf dancing across the grass.

Our goal for the day was to avoid an agenda. We wanted to escape the frantic wedding planning for just a moment, to enjoy each other and the world we lived in. We wanted to maintain a bigger perspective than what was happening in our own little world.

High branches swayed in the wind, sunlight glistening through. We lost ourselves in the rustling pages of books. Sprawled across a blanket, we revisited memories of friends in different states, added more countries to a growing mental list of future travels, confided in each other our doubts and lack of faith.

"Sometimes it's disheartening even to pray," I told her, "because I often lack the feeling of God, whatever that is supposed to feel like."

Maybe you've wanted that feeling, too—proof of your connection with someone. We all want affirmation of things we hold to be true. We want to know if we've found what really matters. I wondered if my love for Kati and her love for me mattered enough to commit our lives to each other, and if our connection would continue even when the feelings didn't.

Talking with Kati that day affirmed the trustworthiness I sought in a partner. Trust is like a beard: it must be gained slowly, but it can be lost quickly. How someone responds to your most vulnerable moments shows how much you can trust that person. It's a good thing God doesn't belittle our desire for feelings and affirmations. I get the sense he likes it, as if we're children tugging at a father's sleeve, then he turns around from his workbench and wraps us in unhindered embrace.

When We Doubt

Despite our frequent lack of faith, God waits for us to catch up. There's a part in the Bible that says, "If we are faithless, he remains faithful, for he cannot disown himself."[89] That's a pretty bold sentiment, about God being so entwined in our affairs that he won't give up on us. He identifies himself so closely with people that he calls them part of himself, as if they're a foreign branch grafted into a tree. The branches just become more of what the tree is already growing into.

Our periods of faithlessness highlight God's forgiveness. Not only does he forgive when we make stupid choices or run away from him; he forgives and works to bring us back in a persistent, caring way.

God's intent was never to make us feel bad about messing up; he always invites us to something better. He wants us to experience the best of life, to thrive in living out our purpose. So as he pursues us, he drops clues about what he's doing, where we can meet up with him and exchange stories over coffee. He offers us moments to find a bit of rest and shut out the rest of the world for a little while. It's often during those refreshing times that we're given renewed perspective, energized for stepping into the next chapter of life, or simply motivated to return to daily routines infused with a little more humble joy.

God pursues us in our frantic attempts to reassemble the lives we once had under control, or thought we did. In the midst of the stress and conflict, he meets with us to refresh and recharge our souls to carry on. God's not surprised by or afraid of our doubts. He loves us despite our reservations. That's the kind of affirming grace he gives, and it's the kind we need when our lives are filled with distracting details, hurried tasks, and lack of focus on the bigger things around us.

I was floored the day I read one counselor's insight about God:

> He won't meet our needs outside of a connection where we have to show up and crack our hearts open to him, because that very connection is what we need to have our needs met in the first place.[90]

God meets us on the grassy slopes, on our picnic blankets in the shade, as we enjoy the world we find ourselves in and dream up the next chapter of our lives in his story.

36

A Package from the Past

"No summer ever came back, and no two summers ever were alike. Times change, and people change; and if our hearts do not change as readily, so much the worse for us."

NATHANIEL HAWTHORNE

When the doorbell rang one August day, I sauntered from my kitchen to open the front door. A large brown box, doused in Oregon morning sunlight, greeted me on the porch. My parents had sent it from the house where I grew up in Minnesota. I rushed the box inside and rustled in a kitchen drawer for my pocketknife—the one from my days on the farm—to open it.

As I dug into the packing peanuts and cut through tape and bubble wrap, the package's contents brought a smile to my face. My father included the *Lord of the Rings* edition of Risk and other board games I played as a teenager. I remembered the scores of late nights with friends, battling with dice and snarky retorts. I unraveled plastic from a couple *Star Wars* models, and I reminisced about my decades-long infatuation with the sci-fi adventure films.

A couple LEGO vehicles triggered memories of countless hours spent on the floor in my childhood bedroom—an adamant introvert's fortress—digging through tubs of bricks for just the right piece. When I unfolded the box's only article of clothing, I nearly high-fived myself. The fifteen-year-old Michael Jordan jersey resurfaced middle school memories of conquest and embarrassment on the court.

I laughed to myself, as if it were the first time I had seen the items of my childhood in a box, each item better than the last. Fond memories of my early years played like a highlight reel in my mind, yet part of me wanted to avoid limiting my life to a collection of a few items.

Anticipation

I don't know anyone who doesn't enjoy receiving a package. The idea of something in the mail with your name on it is part mystery, but undeniably happy. It's the same when you know what's coming—like a party, an anniversary, or a meetup with some friends—and your sense of expectation builds momentum.

If we lived like we expect something good is coming, we might be more available to the people and causes we care about most. We might open our eyes a little wider or listen a little closer. We may even offer our help to new neighbors moving in next door or get to know the quiet person in the corner after a church service, even if we're introverted, too.

It feels inspiring to inspire others. We've each got something to contribute, experiences to share, and things to accomplish. When we choose to be passive and remain comfortable rather than taste new adventures, it's stifling and constricting. There's so much more to life, and we're missing out.

Like many adamant introverts, I'm often calm, calculated, and only selectively excitable. I don't gravitate toward action sports or attending every social event. Some people have the gift of crazy, but I'm usually the one staring at that person in confusion. On the other hand, I have climbed a few modest mountains and went on some canoe trips into the remote lakes of Northern Minnesota. If friends are visiting I stay up later than normal, but I wouldn't pull an all-nighter—except for the time I spontaneously co-hosted a show on the college radio station in the middle of the night. And usually when I know I should eat a salad, I eat another piece of pizza. I feel like a child stuck in a grown-up's body. So I guess I can let go of my reservations a little, in a guarded sort of way.

There's this idea in my head about approaching life with more hopeful expectations, but it doesn't always travel eighteen inches down to my heart to make an impact. Connecting my head and my heart is the only way I can change myself. The unity of body, mind, and spirit sounds so Buddhist and peaceful, but it also sounds like the kind of integration God invites us into.[91]

Sometimes we meet people who strike a healthy balance between childlike enthusiasm and adult responsibility. They're the ones who appear to have their lives on a track to accomplish something big, but they're still open to discarding their plans for a detour in excitement. Even better, the track they're on is what they're actually excited about. It seems too good to be true to have a career, routine, and tasks worth our excitement. But for each of us, there's got to be a path that leads us on the adventure we've always craved, carrying out the responsibility we've been given—a unity of head and heart. Our work is to find it.

Motivation

The box of things from my parents took me back to simpler days, the days of my childhood when everything was stable and familiar. It rekindled the memories of adventures I experienced through the fictional stories of a distant galaxy, and the friends I enjoyed. It brought me back to my roots and how I've remained the same, and it proved how I've changed.

Malcolm Gladwell said, "That's your responsibility as a person, as a human being: to constantly be updating your positions on as many things as possible. And if you don't contradict your-self on a regular basis, then you're not thinking."[92] Challenging your assumptions is a shortcut to growth. The conflict of old ideas against new ones is how you decide what you believe and how you act.

Reminiscing about an important moment or season doesn't have to be only a memory; it can be motivating. Remembering our past encourages us to live fully in the present in hopes that we'll also look back on these days as meaningful experiences.

My friend Christian once said, "Do not let your past hinder a better future, and do not let the future scare you from living out the present." What experiences today do you want to remem-ber decades down the road? The way you live here and now determines how your life will appear looking back.

37

Running from the Nourishment We Need

"In solitude we discover that community is not a common ideology, but a response to a common call."

HENRI NOUWEN

Community used to be a word that always sounded like the right thing to say, but didn't really carry any practical weight. Over time, during college and when I moved back home without a job, it picked up more meaning. Now I can't think of my life without it—staying connected with friends, making new acquaintances, and connecting people from different circles into a new one, while still protecting my times of solitude.

Providing a space for those connections is one of the reasons Kati and I like hosting parties at our home. It's exciting to sit back and see a new face establish common ground with another couple of people, to gain a little more confidence in a new social environment. That's what others provided for us in Oregon, and we want to pass it on.

For as much as I want to encourage community, I fall short of connecting in it myself. Especially during times that feel like conflict—when a job's demands, volunteer commitments, and general busyness collide together—I'm apt to fall into a lazy routine. It happens to all of us, doesn't it? Comfortable predictability kills good intentions.

Intentions

Being in community, connected to other people, is both a beautiful and frightful thing. It gives everyone the possibility of building more healthy relationships. But there's also social risk because connection requires proximity; the closer you are to something, the more it can affect you and even hurt you. Conflict is an unavoidable byproduct of connecting. Real relationships are always risky. Certainly, you choose wisely which people you surround yourself with, but no matter the social cost—potential embarrassment, vulnerability, or unreciprocated care—we must connect because we are meant to. The conflict is worth facing.

We all crave meaningful connection, but we each handle the conflict of our connections differently. We get disoriented without a network of healthy family, friendships, and acquaintances. I wonder if that's the underlying craving of a cheating spouse or guys going alone to a strip club. Whatever the norm at home is, they've left it behind in search of a more fulfilling interaction. There are whole layers of sexuality and psychology in that sort of thing, but it seems that the craving for connection burrows deep among the roots of those actions. Whatever connection he's getting isn't enough; *there's got to be more*, he says.

Some days I'm a self-blinded hypocrite, like someone who talks about healthy living but eats dessert with every meal. I say I value community, but then in social situations I find myself compulsively checking my phone for new messages or social media posts from strangers across the continent, oblivious to the people across the table from me, in the same room, in the same city. And in those moments, I know I have to change.

Nourishment

I heard a sermon about the necessity of relationships a few

years ago. The pastor cautioned against the seclusion that laziness and comfort provide. He said, as if directly for an introvert like me to hear, that most of us would rather curl up on the couch to watch Netflix than venture into the risky environment of social interaction. After all, television doesn't require much from us. To spend time with living, breathing, messy, imperfect people requires energy and patience, and people are a whole lot more unpredictable than an evening on the couch. People have needs. Television can't look me in the eyes and ask for help. I can turn the TV off when I'm bored with it, but I can't do that with people (though there are times I would like to). Perhaps for you, it's browsing Facebook or Instagram, a video game, home projects, or something else.

It would be nice to skip out on spending time with people when there are so many movies I haven't seen and good books waiting on my bookshelf. Madeleine L'Engle captured it when she wrote, "I do face facts. They're lots easier to face than people, I can tell you."[93] There's so much to do besides connect, but information and entertainment will always be there. People won't.

When I realize I've spent a week's worth of evenings perusing Twitter feeds rather than sharing a conversation with a few friends over dinner and drinks, those moments are mired in regret. I missed out on something good for me. Even introverts need a cycle of recharging and reconnection.

The challenge for introverts is not to become less introverted; it is to choose times to lean toward people because isolation isn't healthy or sustainable, even though many of us are drawn to it. For extroverts, the challenge may be to occasionally lean into solitude to develop deeper self-reflection and less dependence on the approval or presence of others. We need a rhythm of recharging in solitude and engaging in community, neither at the expense of the other.

There's something distinctly powerful about sharing food

with other people. Even the image of individuals coming together to enjoy something, to be nourished and sustained together for another day, is beautiful. It nods at something bigger than the meal, and bigger even than the people.

I remember reading a book one night in my college dorm room, and one line jumped off the page and lodged in my brain: "As Christians, it is our duty to master the art of the long meal."[94]

It seemed funny to me at first. I thought, *Doesn't God want us to be productive, and use our time wisely? Shouldn't we just eat quick meals so we can get on to other, more spiritual things?* But I realized that being with people is using our time wisely, and taking time to connect with each other is profoundly spiritual. The point of the long meal is to share time and food and ourselves with others across the table. A rushed meal doesn't provide much space for honest connection between two or four or ten people. A long meal requires conversation, *how are yous*, questions, answers, and tangents. And where people share a bit of themselves with someone else, there is room for flourishing.

I love what author Shauna Niequist wrote in her book, *Bread & Wine:*

> The heart of hospitality is about creating space for someone to feel seen and heard and loved. It's about declaring your table a safe zone, a place of warmth and nourishment. Part of that, then, is honoring the way God made our bodies, and feeding them in the ways they need to be fed.[95]

The Gospel accounts in the Bible are like one long progressive dinner with Jesus and a revolving assortment of dinner guests. Sometimes it was the down-and-out crowd; other times it was the religious leaders. Uncomfortably, it was often a mixture of people from different social groups. Most of the time his best friends were there with him. Those friends of Jesus were some of the first to acknowledge him as the son of God, as the healer and rescuer they'd waited for. Those friends shared so many meals with Jesus, traveled so far with him, observed his actions, and talked with him—those men and women who would change the world.

The more you get to know Jesus, the more you'll see how much God values community. He wants people connected to other people, but not cordially or superficially. He wants pockets of people to know each other at the gut level, authentically and deeply, creating space for each other to show up with all their passions, wounds, doubts, and dreams. It's as if God is saying, through the life of Jesus and the stories he's writing in us, that he wants to nourish and heal the world, starting with the people around the table. We get to be a part of it, together.

MOVEMENT FOUR

Integration

38

The Fleeting Moment

*"A person who...does not regard music as a marvelous
creation of God, must be a clodhopper indeed and does not
deserve to be called a human being; he should be permitted to
hear nothing but the braying of asses and the grunting of hogs."*

MARTIN LUTHER

Kati and I saw a live performance the summer we were engaged. The concert was held at an outdoor venue nestled in the
forested hills of historic Jacksonville, Oregon. The band was
called fun. and tickets were sold out, so we stood outside the
fence behind the crowds.

That night, as we took long strides up the hill behind the venue's grassy amphitheater and sipped our iced coffees, purple
and yellow light washed against the tall pines and the darken-
ing sky. As was our tendency, we exchanged pun-riddled jokes,
including the name fun. in as many punch lines as we could
think up. Stars shone in rebellion against the technical production, not caring that floodlights and haze accompanied the
sounds emanating from the stage. It was quite a place to experience the energy of live music, the strange collision of nature
and technology right out in the mountains of the Northwest.

Part of what makes live music richer than recorded music,
in some ways, is the phenomenon of one-time improvisations.
Unlike a recording of our favorite song we listen to repeatedly,

a live song dwells in the moment. The slight change in a guitar solo or including a cappella choruses only happen at that show, that night, from the whims of the artists. Attendees soak in the experience, believing they are an essential part of it, as if making a history of their own.

When I played in a band during high school and college, I was always more nervous singing or strumming a guitar during a recording session than performing at a concert. The concert was just temporary; people would sing along and mostly remember how the music made them feel or the good time they had with their friends in the front row. A recording could be listened to hundreds and thousands of times, with much higher expectations for musical precision and consistency. I didn't want to release a recording of a half-hearted harmony or lackluster guitar solo. Listening to recordings on a computer or smartphone doesn't offer the luxury of distraction from an imperfect note, like watching a live band dance around on stage.

The Magic of Music

There's something mystical about a live performance. The crowd murmurs with anticipation, stage set and lights low. Leading figures take the stage, but not before their reputations preceding them.

The lights burst out of the darkness with the strike of the first chord. Melodies soar, exuding passion from the stage that oozes into the front rows and makes its way to the back. A lyrical hook captivates the room. Hundreds or thousands of voices join in unison, proclaiming some strange verse in musical poetry.

Though merely one in a crowd of many, a person can get caught up in the reverie of the music, the performance, and the moment. Music has a magical way of bringing people together. From across backgrounds and various professions and different worldviews and social classes, songs create unity. Music lends itself to spiritual experience. All become one, even if just for a moment.

In live music, artistic demonstrations, dramas, or any number of performances, people savor a taste of something bigger than themselves. Other concerns fade out of focus as a story is told or sung. Our conflicts pause: anxiety recedes, temporarily forgetting the strained family life waiting at home, the pressures of a job, or fears about the unforeseen variables we'll inevitably encounter. Those are very real concerns, but the crescendos and lyrics swelling around us are what matter right now, in this moment.

Music gives the soul language to express the inexpressible. Notes and tempos build a plateau on which all sorts of thinkers, dreamers, pessimists, and optimists gather to tap into a force otherwise inaccessible. We thrive on that inspiration. One writer discovered, "Art and love are the same thing: It's the process of seeing yourself in things that are not you."[96]

Our spirits drink up lyrics in rhyme like dry ground soaks up the spring rain. How strangely beautiful that music can access part of our inner selves we seldom give one another.

Presence

Kati and I walked back to the car when the performance concluded, weaving through crowds that flooded Jacksonville's narrow residential streets. Melodies from the concert resonated in our minds, endearing the band's appeal to our senses as live performances often do. I took only a couple unimpressive, poorly lit photos of fun.'s show with my phone. I didn't need great pictures of the experience I had because I was with Kati, spoke with her, and laughed with her. Our bad jokes and humming along with the melody sufficed as memories of that day, ways we found to express part of the inexpressible. We were learning to experience more of life together, not wishing circumstances were just a little bit different or trying to capture perfect moments to post on a Facebook page.

It's easy to dwell in the past or anticipate the future, but the present offers plenty for us in the meantime. Few easy things are the best things, but staying engaged in every fleeting moment matters. Real life happens only once; we'd best pay attention. Before we know it, the moment's passed and a new one greets us.

39

The Pressures of Marriage

"The primary problem is...learning how to love and care for the stranger to whom you find yourself married."

STANLEY HAUERWAS

After another night of wedding planning with Kati during our engagement, we still had a mountain of details to organize. Some of those nights left us in a state of apathy and defeat.

We were only months away from having all those catering options and venue bills behind us, but the commiserating only added to the stress. Days and days dragged on, and weeks felt void of progress. We needed direction, but we failed to latch on to something outside ourselves.

The Thing About Marriage

When I was single, there was a temptation to think of marriage as a goal. It was supposed to guarantee we'd never be lonely. But human affection, though wonderful and intoxicating on its own, isn't enough to satisfy our souls.

Being married isn't some goal to be achieved; it's a dynamic, transformative commitment to stay connected to another human, regardless of circumstances or feelings. We think the wedding is the most important event of our lives until we're married and we realize it's a daily necessity to choose love.

Love is always a choice; that's what makes it so powerful.

Marriage is the beginning of a new chapter—an entirely different book, really. It's a book bound in love and forgiveness and late nights, knowing smiles, dirty dishes, future hopes, broken dreams, and renewed faith. It's a book many start, but not everyone finishes. I'm told there are often sad chapters—depressing, hollow, and lackluster. But through and through, it's meant to be a quietly confident story that opens eyes to fresh beauty.

I haven't been married for long, but I've got this theory: a marriage does best when it's not focused on being a good marriage.

Relationships are designed to thrive on something beyond the people involved. If the purpose of the relationship is to be a good relationship, they will feel like failures for a large amount of the time because disagreements seep in and conflict threatens the stability of the connection.

Conflict is inevitable because the world is broken and people are broken. We each want what's best for ourselves, even at the expense of those around us. Though kindness is possible, self-centeredness is human nature from cradle to grave, from childhood playgrounds to corporate ladders. Marriage isn't conflict-proof, either—it's intensified. The closer people get to each other, the more damage conflict can do.

One pastor I know has learned a lot from marriage. He told me during the ten years he's been married, he is confronted time and again with the fact that he is fundamentally selfish. He said it only amplified with the addition of children.

If my friend realized he's even more selfish than he thought, I think we're all pretty selfish because he's a pastor and even he knows he's selfish.

Marriage is one of the most demanding roles of a person's life because it requires resilience and self-sacrifice. Selflessness is a risky challenge but a noble one, because giving away part of your life has the power to enhance someone else's. Living in close quarters with a spouse for years and years reveals the caliber of a person's character. And most married couples I know admit their spouses have plenty of room for improvement, even if they're still crazy in love.

If marriage is like a pressure cooker for two selfish people, it's bound to face plenty of conflict. When a couple tries to focus on being in a good marriage, they'll unintentionally adopt a sense of failure the moment there's friction. They feel incapacitated by the weight of conflict, even though the disagreements and stress are completely natural.

A marriage will implode on itself when counting on its own success and happiness. If the relationship is committed to something else, however, the higher purpose gives the conflict new meaning. Disagreements are no longer grounds for dismissing the relationship, but opportunities for the connection to deepen as both parties pursue a purpose bigger than themselves. Contracts fall apart when people change their minds, but a covenant remains because it's a commitment to something greater.

Front-Row Seat

When God performed the Bible's first wedding, between Man and Woman in the Garden of Eden, he showed what kind of purpose marriage is made for. God had given Man a task to accomplish—to cultivate the Garden, bring order, and produce more life—but there was something more than that. Everything God created he declared good, yet the first thing God declared not good wasn't a disorganized garden, but a lonely human.[97]

God wasn't only concerned about what Man could do, but also cared about whom he was with.

The purpose of marriage isn't found in what two people can do for each other; it's in who they're becoming together. It's a passionate friendship built on remaining by each other's side no matter what. It's a declaration to choose each other every day, because that's what love does. Marriage is a front-row seat to see the redemptive work God is doing in your partner.

We can learn to love how God is changing someone like we learn to love a person in the first place. We don't just marry our spouses as they are, but who they're becoming and who they will be. Through all our striving and growing and changing, we love most profoundly when we care for and enhance each other like Jesus cares for and enhances his people, the church.[98]

Pastor Tim Keller explains it like this:

> What happens if we see the mission of marriage to teach us about our sins in unique and profound ways and to grow us out of them through providing someone who speaks the truth in love to us? How different it would be if we were to fall in love especially with the glorious thing God is doing in our spouse's life?[99]

Speaking the truth in love sounds so tidy and achievable, but I've seen a lot of relationships that aren't on that page. Some days my marriage doesn't even have that on the radar. The sad truth is that many marriages become about self-fulfillment—the money or the kids, control or security—or they cease to exist at all.

Why Marriage?

I've heard preachers say marriage is about both happiness and holiness. It seems true, though I'm still learning what that looks like in flesh and blood. I get the happiness part, that we can find incredible joy in connection with someone.

The holiness part is the mysterious half, but I think it's tied closely to character. No one can deliver on the promise of an easy life—just one full of variables, defining challenges, and unforeseen rewards. Yet those conflicts are the places in which we learn the most about ourselves, about what's true, and about God. As we venture into new territory with God and a devoted partner, we develop the kind of character that outlasts the easy seasons and sustains us in the darkest ones.

If marriage becomes about only happiness, the relationship will crumble under seasons of suffering and pain. If marriage is about only developing one's own character, two partners will miss out on the gift of each other. The relationship tends to stabilize when both spouses bring their full selves into full connection, living full of purpose.

Marriage is the most durable when it's about both joy and character. Happiness and holiness work together on the fulcrum of marriage, not necessarily to bring a perfect balance, but to bring a mutually sustainable entity that wouldn't otherwise be possible. Author Sarah Bessey wrote, "Marriage is a beautiful example of oneness and cooperation, an image of the dance of the Trinity in perfect unity."[100] In the end, marriage is about two becoming one because they're better together.

How Love Changes

The best marriages are ones that look effortless, but you know their story: how they met young, suffered miscarriages and rebellious children, sustained each other through lost jobs and poor health. Their kind of love is a miracle, and you get the sense that all relationships could be great if more people held love like that—pulsing with life like philosopher Kahlil Gibran described: "Love one another, but make not a bond of love: Let it rather be a moving sea between the shores of your souls."[101] And you believe that your marriage and your relationships can be better than they are right now, if only you could grow that kind of sturdy, knock-down, drag-out love. You and your spouse would overflow with so much resilient commitment and grace that you couldn't help but share it with those around you.

Marriage is a picture of how love changes people. It's a story God still writes today, and he invites us into it with the choices we make and the people we surround ourselves with. Commitment teaches us to choose love, day in and day out. Love is the power that God uses to shape us, and he loves who we're becoming.

40

Facing Our Flaws

"Reflect upon your present blessings—of which every man has many—not on your past misfortunes, of which all men have some."
CHARLES DICKENS

The older I get, the more aware of my flaws I become.

Inadequacy is a ghost. It haunts us all in different ways, whether tied to failures of our past, fears of our future, or the circumstances we're in. We simply don't think we have what it takes to meet the expectations of others—or worse, of ourselves.

You've felt it, too, haven't you? We're meant for more than we're currently living, but we don't think we have the tools to figure out the next step. The gnawing feeling that we're not enough especially shows up in relationships and work, paralyzing our efforts in self-fulfilling prophecy.

It's not pleasant to be reminded of our flaws. Even the most well-adjusted among us tends to evade the spotlight of authenticity when it threatens to reveal our blemishes. We can bear it for a while, but sooner or later we'll collapse for lack of living up to the truth. The truth is a powerful thing; sooner or later, it finds us out. Like a dazzling sunset nestled in the clouds after a summer storm, our eyes can't look away. It's written all over the sky.

Seeing the reality of our weaknesses prompts us to look beyond ourselves. When we lack something, we seek satisfaction elsewhere. Our imperfection redirects our curiosity toward what's perfect.

Intervention

Great stories show the human struggle against our own imperfections. Before he became the church leader we think of today, Paul was a person of prominent standing in social, political, and religious spheres. He found great happiness in the high rankings of his religious life, until Jesus appeared to him in a vision and told him the plan had changed.[102]

Saul—his name before it changed to Paul—was headed from Jerusalem to the Syrian town of Damascus, on orders from religious leaders to imprison or kill anyone who threatened the religious rituals and systems in place. A sect of Judaism had split off into something called The Way, with followers declaring the laws and prophecies of the Old Testament had taken a new meaning. They insisted that a man named Jesus, who was killed by the Roman authorities and religious leaders, had come back from the dead and was the leader they'd been waiting for.

Saul's Jewish faith and temple-based religious system perceived The Way as a threat to the status quo, especially since the Roman military occupying Israel was quick to use deadly force against people who called anyone but Caesar king.

The road Saul walked would've taken him to imprison and kill those who didn't believe what he believed—people who believed in Jesus and started living differently because of it. Saul considered himself justified in doing so, even blessed by his religious system. It was work that would boost his social and religious credibility to the people he wanted to impress. But God, because he had a better plan, stopped him on the road and changed him. Jesus met him there, gave him a new purpose, a new story, and a new name: terrorist Saul became Apostle Paul.

A New Path

We're all on a road to somewhere, walking a path toward something better—or so we hope. Just as Jesus stopped Paul on his path, Jesus breaks into our lives to reset our direction and create a new chapter within our story. Sometimes God needs to save us from ourselves, from our shortsighted, foolish desires and selfish ambitions. Sometimes we just need a little morale boost to keep going. Other times, we need help pulling a 180-degree turn and getting back to what God called us to.

God is one who intervenes. He has intervened throughout history, and he continues to intervene in moments of conflict to protect his people, reveal himself to skeptics, and incite good in the world.

Even though God intervened in Paul's journey of prideful, hate-filled religion, he didn't heal Paul and send him off all at once. The story goes on to explain Paul's temporary blindness until God used another person to instruct him in the new path he was to walk. This new path was one of humility: God said he had a special role for Paul, and sent him to share the message of love and redemption with people considered unqualified to associate with God.[103] The very people Paul's former religious system sought to destroy then became his coworkers in sharing the message of The Way—the story of Jesus.

Over the years that followed, Paul obeyed God's calling to this new role and faced great resistance from those who led the religious system he used to uphold. Even while enduring social rejection, imprisonment, beatings, and harmful persecution, something else ate away at Paul. Scholars aren't entirely sure what he meant, but Paul wrote about something he called a "thorn in my flesh," which kept him from becoming conceited.[104]

Whatever the "thorn in my flesh" was, Paul knew it was as much about a spiritual condition as it was a physical ailment.

He asked God to remove it three times, but God responded: "My grace is sufficient for you, for my power is made perfect in weakness."[105]

The new measure of Paul's life was accepting his own weakness in light of God's sufficiency. God's strength was revealed where Paul lacked it, so God got the credit for Paul's accomplishments. Whatever vexed him also kept him humble and dependent on God as the source of his strength and purpose.

In a world that shunned paradoxes and associated vulnerability with shame, Paul wrote, with a heart transformed by grace and truth: "For when I am weak, then I am strong."[106]

Journals

One of the ways I realize the flaws of my past—and present—is by reading my journals. Digging out the fake leather-bound books and old college-ruled notebooks conjures memories of years gone by. The pages revisit the thoughts and desires that consumed my life a decade ago, a month ago, and everywhere in between. I learned, like G. K. Chesterton explained:

> You have to be happy in those quiet moments when you remember that you are alive; not in those noisy moments when you forget. Unless we can learn again to enjoy life, we shall not long enjoy the spices of life.[107]

Every so often, I excavate stacks of journals from the closet and sit on the floor as I flip through their pages. I could pass hours like that, and sometimes I do when it's drizzling all day in Southern Oregon and the calendar provides no reason to outrun the comforts of introversion. Journals are time machines, transporting me back into exact places and experiences with people and a mind swarming with ideas.

As a middle school kid, I got the impression it was good to keep a record of what I read in the Bible and the things I prayed about. Though a rigid ritual at first, that became the start of something more valuable than I could have ever imagined, although the form shifted several times from year to year. I started adding questions and doubts about the things I read, and in college included details about people, places, and conversations that shifted my worldview.

With these sections of each daily entry, my journal became even more useful in tracking how far I'd come in body, mind, and spirit. Sometimes the growth was negative. The journal also revealed how much I still lacked. As I flip back six months or a couple years in the pages, I'm a bit embarrassed to remember how many times I had to hear the same truths.

The brazen authenticity of knowing your own past—that's both the blessing and the curse of journaling. I cannot change what I did, the ideas I held, or the failures I experienced those years ago. My old self is stuck in the past, frozen in the unchanging state of unusable humiliation. But on the bright side, my old self is stuck in the past, and I am always adapting with each new page I add to this variable life.

I don't have to be ashamed of my past because my life today looks much different than it used to. If I were in the same place I was in six months or three years or a decade ago, that would be cause for serious concern—lifeless, unmoving. We are meant to grow. We were designed with an unrelenting need to reshape our existence. Danish philosopher Søren Kierkegaard knew: "Now with God's help, I shall become myself."[108]

You can't live in the past, but you can learn from it. Enjoy the good stories from it. Laugh at the mistakes of your past, because your future isn't bound to the same things if you seek a new way of living. You can find forgiveness and second chances if you acknowledge you don't have it all together. Through honest humility, you find redemption. Second chances plot the course to a healthier variable life. It's never too late to change the direction of your story.

The same Jesus who transformed Paul's story also intervenes on the paths of our lives today. And like Jesus told Paul, he says he has not given up on us. He knows the darkness we've been through and the happiness we've sought in the wrong places. He's well acquainted with our weaknesses, because he's been walking with us all along. Yet still he says, "My grace is sufficient for you, for my power is made perfect in weakness." That kind of power changes everything we see and how we see it.

41

Seeing Through Screens

*"We desire connection and community in our increasingly
nomadic existence—yet we wander around the globe, glancing off
other digital nomads without ever knowing or being known."*

SHANE HIPPS

An article in the *New York Times* cited a fascinating study about people and technology. The study found when people sit down to dinner with each other but keep their phones in reach, they're more likely to keep the conversation shallow so they can dip in and out while scrolling through news feeds or text messages. Even when two people set their phones on the table or in their peripheral vision, it limited the depth of their conversation as well as their sense of connection.[109] I stood motionless with astonishment for a full minute after I read it. Clearly, our mobile connectivity costs something.

Like my tendency at a live concert or a fun night out with friends, it's tempting to capture the right moment with a photo or check on social media updates. Sometimes it feels like a bad habit I need to kick, the frequent impulse to turn my focus to the little screen in my pocket.

Some decry the potential harm of social media. Since it's such a young branch of technology, we don't yet know what it does to us long-term. Decades before smartphones and Instagram, one author warned how photography takes us out of the moments we're living: "The life that you live in order to photo-graph it is already, at the outset, a commemoration of itself."[110]

Culture trends project that we'll continue getting more and more "social," but at what cost? Everything posted online is ar-chived. Our digital footprint balloons into a lifestyle database, but we barely even stop to consider the legacy our data will convey.

Something is happening to the way we experience life. With the emergence of more and more personalized apps and op-portunities for sharing, we subconsciously view our lives as a series of content rather than a stream of existence.

Rather than an ebbing and flowing existence, anchored deep in relationships and growing through struggle, our lives have become news feeds of only our best content. We might post photos of a trendy pastry shop or brunch place under per-fect lighting and a blurb about catching up with someone we love, just so our followers can see how exotic and connected our lives are. But wouldn't it be better to sit down over coffee and talk honestly with a friend than to merely share it on social media? I'm preaching to myself, too. What if we set aside the screens between us, getting past each other's curated moments to see each other's character? We could share our real selves, highlights and low points and all. I immediately saw this ten-sion when Donald Miller wrote, "If we live behind a mask, we can impress but we can't connect."[111]

Though I still take photos at concerts and tweet my appreci-ation of a restaurant's food or drink, I'm trying to be conscious of the way I allow screens closer access to experiences than I allow myself. Am I trying to capture a moment or am I really dwelling in it? Maybe you've asked yourself that question, and maybe it challenges you the way it challenges me.

The Mint

Relationships keep us grounded in reality. Without community, we get lost in ourselves and our petty little worlds. Our perspectives are challenged, unnecessary ones falling away like autumn leaves, as we allow carefully chosen confidantes to examine and speak to our honest selves.

One of my college roommates was like that. Pat didn't have a smartphone or a Facebook account. I asked him if he was serious when he first said he wasn't on Facebook. He patted his wavy brown hair and adjusted his glasses, then leaned his lanky frame against the loft bed as he explained. Everyone in college was on Facebook. By that time, even high school kids were getting on Facebook, but Pat wasn't.

Pat reasoned he didn't need to spend more time in front of a computer, browsing online. He had enough screen time with his undergrad studies. He wanted to go to law school after getting his degree so he studied a lot, hours every night. Pat was also serious about avoiding wasted time. Rather than play around online, trying to learn about other people like a stalker would, he thought it better to actually spend time with them in person.

Just north of Minneapolis, a few of us split rent in a small house near my college campus. Dan was a musician and filmmaker with blond hair, glasses, and plaid shirts, using animated hand gestures when he spoke. He looked as Scandinavian as anyone you could find in Minnesota, save for old-timers living in remote cabins near the Canadian border. Sometimes Dan played music with Matt, a computer programmer who alternated between a full beard, a mustache, long and wild hair, and a crew cut during the time I lived at that house. We called our home The Mint because that's the shade of green everybody saw as they drove through our neighborhood, even from a few blocks away. And in The Mint, we loved our traditions.

That winter, when the sun went down before five o'clock and the degrees dropped until the snow crunched underfoot, I played Monopoly with Pat, Dan, and Matt. We played late into the night because there was nothing to do when we'd already completed our studies and the outdoors were an unforgiving, barren tundra.

Playing Monopoly on so many winter nights grew to be more fun than any of us expected. It was refreshing to unplug from the digital world for a few hours, downgrading to cardboard and plastic trinkets strewn on a table. Board games are portals to simpler times, as we relearn to look across the table into the eyes of another human being—laughing, convincing, considering other bodies and minds without the barriers of pretense and pixels.

I began to understand what Pat meant about not needing Facebook, that it was just a decoy if its purpose was to connect people. I probably entertained the idea of deleting my account, but it was fleeting. Pat's approach made me reconsider the unnecessary time I spent in front of computers and TVs, and I wanted to trade some of it for meaningful time in front of human beings, even if I was a rather adamant introvert.

Off Screen

When I reflect on my life, the things that have really mattered to me, my memories aren't filled with those times I spent staying up late to stalk Facebook accounts or Instagram feeds. The best memories are moments of reflection and realization in solitude, as well as moments with people, doing something and going somewhere. I remember late-night conversations about theology, beer, and girls; road trips to big cities and concerts; camping near the Minnesota-Canadian border; and drinking hot chocolate with my family by the fireplace.

If I realize what's most important—building healthy relationships with people and building something good in the world— why would I want to replace that with unnecessary time awash in the digital glow? There's got to be a better method of using technology, but not being used by it. We're fools to leave portions of our lives unlived in exchange for empty screen time.

Perhaps there are even parts of our lives left unlived that we've yet to realize were missing. The world waits for us to power down, stand up, and actually connect.

I'll try to take poet Mary Oliver's advice, and I hope you will, too:

> Instructions for living a life:
> Pay attention.
> Be astonished.
> Tell about it.[112]

42

Instagram and the Power of Yes

*"The big question is whether you are going to
be able to say a hearty yes to your adventure."*

JOSEPH CAMPBELL

There are plenty of downsides and distractions provided by
technology, but there are incredible benefits, too.

Kati and I took a couple days off in the winter. Our routines
drudged on after Christmas and the New Year, taking their
wearying toll on our schedules and energy. We were eager
for the chance to get out of town and experience the adventures provided by new scenery. Since I'd finally upgraded to an
iPhone the year before, I was eager to use more apps and social
media on the go, especially Instagram.

Going Social

Within a few years of their creation, social networks have
flourished because they tap into something at the core of humanity: we are made for connection. It's easy to use them for
vain self-promotion, but the underlying appeal is that desire to
connect. People are meant to interact, like individual pieces of
a puzzle begging to be put together so something bigger and
more beautiful comes into focus.

I was intrigued by the way people came together over beautiful images and sincere captions on Instagram, though there's a lot of the opposite to avoid. It wasn't long before I learned about InstaMeets, a meet-up of users in a city to connect with each other in person. As I learned more about Instagram and found more talented photographers to fill my feed, I realized its power as a social network.

It began when I found high-quality photos by a few people my friends knew. Several of the best photographers were based in Portland, including one whose name sounded familiar. His username was @colincabalka.

People like @colincabalka seemed really good-natured and kind, always promoting someone else's photos and posting well-written thoughts about making the most of life, doing good, and being curious about how God fit into everything. When I heard about InstaMeets, I wondered if any of the people I followed would be willing to meet in person.

When Kati and I made travel arrangements to visit Portland, I summoned a bit of courage to ask a few of the people on Instagram if they'd like to meet up. It felt sort of like arranging a blind date: I had no idea what to expect. Their photos seemed pretty normal, but there was still a miniscule chance they could be psychopaths posing as really good smartphone photographers.

Despite my rather adamant introvert tendencies to avoid foreign social experiences, something in me kept saying yes. There's a certain kind of power in saying yes to something or someone. It opens up a world of possibility that would otherwise remain closed because of a no. Saying yes affords us the adventures that help define us, deepen our character, and make us more like the people God designed us to be.

I made the ask with an Instagram comment, and @colincabalka responded with an invitation to breakfast he hosted with a few guys every Thursday. I told Kati I was considering sharing a meal with total strangers in a private residence early in the morning. She told me to go for it, but that she would gladly sleep in while I ventured into this uncharted social territory. (Sometimes she's an even more adamant introvert than I am.)

InstaWelcome #1

Kati and I arrived in Portland. After a night's rest on the plush hotel bed, I awoke well before sunrise, got ready, and exited the hotel lobby into the cool Northwest winter air. I merged onto the highway, continued several miles, and reached the apartment complex outside the city as the sun began to rise.

I parked and walked up to the address @colincabalka provided, and paused a moment to breathe deeply before I knocked on the door. After a second or two, the door swung open to reveal a few men about my age standing in the entryway.

"Is this where a Colin Cabalka lives?" I asked, doing my best to hide my timidity.

A person with short, wavy brown hair and a lively grin emerged from the kitchen to introduce himself. "John! Welcome, man. Come here!"

He offered a brotherly hug, like we'd known each other for years. "Nice to meet you. I'm Colin. Meet these other guys."

In that bizarre moment, @colincabalka became Colin, a real person with a body and a handshake and friends to introduce. Instead of the virtual front porch of Instagram, we interacted in a warm apartment living room. Instead of gathering over photographs on a smartphone screen, we gathered over French toast, breakfast burritos, and hand-brewed coffee.

During that morning, six or eight guys joined before heading off to work and meetings. Minute by minute, each of us grew more awake with the flavorful coffee, rising sun, and opportunity for dialogue. Colin was passionate about embracing challenges and simple luxuries, and he asked about the conflicts and transitions we each faced.

Another guy had also met Colin and the others through Instagram. He wondered whether God would help his budding career in photography and guide his relationship with his fiancée, to whom he'd just proposed the night prior.

Another fellow told us about an experience he had when he felt God clearly told him to never again make a decision based on money, but to trust in him. He said he's never regretted taking that step forward, keeping faith in the God who has promised to provide.

His friend resonated with that idea and explained how he and his wife were learning to trust God with everything—not just talking about trust, but living in it. The third guy said it was vital for them to be content with what God provided, especially as freelance projects were a little scarce when they started up their own photography and video production company. Each of the young men around the room embodied the aspiration, "Creativity's for others. It's not for yourself; it's to serve others."[113]

As breakfast concluded, we prayed for each other and said our goodbyes. I exchanged contact information with a few of them so we could connect on social media, which seemed a little backwards after what we'd just experienced.

Sitting down over breakfast with complete strangers wasn't so awkward or socially scary after all. In fact, I found some of them quite relatable. We may not have known each other existed before that day, but it was like we were already connected when we walked into that apartment.

God has a funny way of putting people in our path—people who need love and people who give love. Over a meal and conversation, I think every person in that room felt encouraged. It's hard to stay apathetic when you're around someone inspiring. The chemistry of passionate people living with purpose can change not just what you see, but how you think.

That's a key to living well: to stay inspired and surround

yourself with people and ideas that inspire you. Keep saying yes to the best things. Maybe you're inspired by art and beauty, or by finding something wrong in the world and setting it right. Maybe it's exploring new parts of a city or the outdoors, building something with your hands, or new social opportunities that light your fire. Whatever it takes, stay inspired. However you can, use that inspiration to inspire others, too. Saying yes isn't just an answer to a question, but it's a vehicle to take you further on the journey of your variable life.

It's amazing that one little app can lay the foundation for something worthwhile instead of mere self-promotion and entertainment. The power of social media isn't just that it connects people digitally from afar; it's powerful because it can connect people in real, three-dimensional life. Those connections make a tangible difference.

InstaWelcome #2

Six weeks later, Kati and I returned to Portland for another weekend getaway. I arranged to meet up with Colin again, and he kindly invited us to his apartment for coffee.

Earlier that morning, I contacted another Portland Instagrammer, @brandenharvey, whom I'd exchanged messages with online for the better part of a year. I told him we would be glad to meet if he was available, so Kati and I picked him up on the way to Colin's.

When Branden walked out toward the car, he greeted us with a friendly handshake and warm smile. His bright demeanor and signature styled hair—one big, blond curl right above his forehead—contrasted against the dreary Northwest winter sky. He was a living, breathing, happy, authentic person, no longer just a face in a profile picture.

Branden told us stories about spur-of-the-moment camping trips when he slept in the bed of a truck with friends, and how he was learning to use his photography to help others and celebrate good in the world. I wondered why more people weren't like Branden: good at what they do and good to people around them.

The three of us drove to Colin's apartment, where he giddily welcomed us with handshakes and friendly hugs as the smell of freshly poured coffee drifted. Branden and Colin had known each other for a while, connected through social media and mutual friends. I introduced Kati to Colin, and he responded with as much enthusiasm and hospitality as he had treated me with just weeks before.

Colin's roommate was also there. I recognized @ipratt from Instagram, but now he was Ian: tall with neat, dark hair and a sly smile, eager to greet these new faces in his apartment.

As Colin brewed coffee in the kitchen and filled a mug for each of us, we asked Ian about his life in Portland. He was leaving the next day for Uganda, where he would film a humanitarian organization working for human rights and education. It was clear Ian wasn't one to sit around, waiting for life to happen for him. His sharp eyes conveyed flashes of hope for the world and clarity about his work while he spoke. I liked him right away.

The guys asked Kati more about herself, then grew curious about how we met. I smirked toward Kati and shared the beginning of our story, how we crossed paths when I first moved to Oregon and how we'd talked about travel and books. And of course, *The John Weirick Slow Play*.

Kati rolled her eyes playfully, as she always does when I mention *The Slow Play*. Not to be dismayed, I unfolded the story of how we got to know each other over coffee and hiking trails, and eventually realized we were a great match.

We continued the conversation on couches in the small living room, as morning light grew stronger through the sliding glass door. Colin told us about his choice to move from Los Angeles to Portland a year earlier to pursue more connections in the film industry. He'd also moved to Portland to be near a girl who became his girlfriend and then his wife.

Each of those young men wanted to grow beyond themselves, to cultivate their skills and be better people. Maybe I was drawn to them because I knew I needed to do the same.

After refilling our coffee, the conversation meandered into jokes about our pet peeves, then into the internal conflicts that held us back. I shared one of my frustrations: when people don't seem to do anything productive. I asked their advice in helping others move forward and make progress in work, develop a proactive perspective, and grow healthy relationships. They spoke about kindness and patience, the need to extend grace like God extends grace to us, but also call people to something bigger. They were the words I needed to hear in that moment, soothing my spirit with a clarity I was learning to grasp wherever I found it.

Before the group dispersed, we stood in the middle of the room and prayed for each other. We prayed for staying productive in work that mattered, for being lovers of God and of people around us, and for being rooted by faith in the one who provides every good thing.

We said our goodbyes and drove Branden back to his apartment. As he stepped out of the car, he said, "So good to meet you, John and Kati. I'm already looking forward to next time."

Kati moved into the front seat, and we drove away in search of late morning brunch. "I'm glad we met them," she said reassuringly.

I looked over and nodded, thankful for the brief company of digital acquaintances who became real, live friends—grateful for Kati next to me, too, and the richness she added to the adventures I craved.

Life-Giving

I have to tell you one of the things I admire about those guys. They're talented photographers and filmmakers, and they each have an amazing way of telling stories and shedding light on subjects in a way that few others can. They care deeply about art and excellence, and they use their platforms to share vivid depictions of beauty, stories of struggle and hope, pointing to the God behind it all. They've grown large followings online— not just because of their stunning photos, but also because they are learning to do what is life-giving and to be life-giving.

Being around driven, inspired souls does something to re-kindle my own. I sense a deeper conviction to live purposeful-ly, engaging life with honesty and humility. Those guys under-stand that, because they're on the same path.

It's amazing what a couple hours with flavorful, hand-brewed coffee and sincere conversation can do for a person. We find something worthwhile when smartphones are set down and computers are turned off because they've done what they were meant to do in the first place: connect person to person.

43

Sleeping Through the American Dream

"The dangerous assumption we unknowingly accept in the American Dream is that our greatest asset is our own ability."

DAVID PLATT

In the ancient world, followers of Jesus caught a lot of trouble from the powers that dominated the first and second centuries AD. The movement of Christianity across cultures and ethnicities caused a stir in the cultural, religious, and political systems of the day. Many were upset to hear of a king with broader jurisdiction than Caesar, and of a kingdom that called them to selfless nonviolence and reconciliation instead of oppression and conquest.

Many followers of Jesus were mocked and even assaulted to the point of injury or death, but persecution didn't stop them from holding on to the promise Jesus offered: a life of purpose and hope through connection to God. As a leader of Christians in that tumultuous period, Paul wrote about it like this:

> We are hard pressed on every side, but not crushed; perplexed, but not in despair; persecuted, but not abandoned; struck down, but not destroyed. We always carry around in our body the death of Jesus, so that the life of Jesus may also be revealed in our body. For we who are alive are always being given

over to death for Jesus' sake, so that his life may also be revealed in our mortal body. So then, death is at work in us, but life is at work in you.[114]

I'm not sure I understand everything going on here, about carrying the death of Jesus and all, but it's clear Paul believed this: by enduring conflict, they became the kind of people God designed them to be. Something divine and revitalizing showed up in their humanity as they embraced their identity: belonging to the God who made them and called them to a greater purpose.

Life, Liberty, and the Pursuit of Emptiness

Nate says the not-so-middle-class, not-so-comfortable Jesus we read about in the Bible is a difficult pill for modern American Christians to swallow. One scholar said, "We have merged the promise of the gospel with the American dream, and the big task is to pull those two things apart, which of course people resist."[115] So at the risk of facing resistance, let's dig into it for a moment and see if we can separate the two.

Peculiarly, Americans celebrate the right to "life, liberty, and the pursuit of happiness."[116] The life and liberty parts seem valuable for a healthy society. Most of us would agree the baseline of humanitarian values is to not kill or harm another person. Freedom provides an open environment in which individuals can choose to do what they wish, provided they don't infringe on the life or liberty of anyone else. In an ideal world, freedom allows each of us to work on something meaningful that makes life better for everyone. In reality, freedom is typically used to manipulate others to work on what will make life better for us.

The pursuit of happiness, though, is a funny phrase. It seems so intangible. I suppose it refers to the way in which people apply their freedom to do what makes them happy, but the functional translation of the pursuit of happiness has become that everyone ought to live the American Dream.

The Problem with the American Dream

At its core, there is a problem with the American Dream. The American Dream says that to be a true citizen of the land of the free and the home of the brave, one must live with relentless zeal in chasing success, prosperity, self-sufficiency through hard work, and upward mobility (which I like to pretend means being able to fly, but is really less fantastic than that).

The American Dream praises those who have a picture-perfect spouse (who may or may not be sincerely happy); go into debt to live in a sizable home surrounded by a white picket fence; own at least one new SUV and a shiny sedan in the garage; have 2.5 children in the second- or third-floor bedrooms; drive from their home in the suburbs to the children's school for soccer practice, dance recital, and parent-teacher conferences; stay home every night to watch mindless TV after long days at professional jobs of corporate ladder-climbing; do grocery shopping at big box department stores; and go to the lake with the boat on weekends.

Most of the American Dream can be lived largely separated from everyone else. We rarely try to make anything better in the world because we're too busy building our own little kingdoms in our own socio-economic enclaves. In this kind of routine, people can become distractions rather than human beings to know and appreciate. *There's always work and play to keep me busy,* we say. *Why bother with other people? People are messy and require time and patience. It's better just to avoid them— those distractions from my life.*

The philosophy of the American Dream is to create and manage a comfortable life. I don't know if that's written anywhere as the official mission statement of the American Dream, but that's at the heart of building a life to fit inside prescribed boundaries and cultural expectations.

When we first got married, Kati and I discovered we had inadvertently fallen into a sort of American Dream lifestyle. We had a modest house with a white fence around the front yard, and even a two-car garage for our two vehicles (though we're fairly certain the neighborhood was home to minor drug trafficking and a shady party scene—everyone's American Dream is a little different, I suppose). Sometimes we even shopped at department stores stocked high with things we didn't need and watched movies on our flat-screen TV instead of welcoming some new friends over for dinner, drinks, and sharing stories. We got into a comfortable rhythm.

My point is not to call all these things bad; in fact, a lot of these things can be good in the proper context. They aren't inherently problematic unless this sort of lifestyle defines us more than anything else. The American Dream isn't meant to become our identity; it's full of big and prosperous notions, but it's too small. When our perspective of a meaningful life becomes a cookie-cutter imitation of a national philosophy, we lose out on being uniquely ourselves. It's a dangerous thing when a system supplants an individual's identity. The empires of earth insist we pledge allegiance, but our citizenship belongs to a selfless king and a heavenly kingdom.[117]

Throughout the stories of the Bible, God's message is this: *I don't need you to live up to certain ideals, perform rituals, or have your life all put together. I'm more interested in knowing you, personally and honestly; none of those labels or system-bound details define you.*[118]

God doesn't see numbers in systems; he sees faces, personalities, dreams, and fears. We tend to zoom out and categorize groups of people, but God gets up close to each human heart.

In our pursuit to live well, conflict is never totally absent. Try as you might, it's not a matter of escaping discomfort, awkwardness, and pain—that's impossible, anyway. If you're willing to reframe your perspective, however, you can face conflict with a greater sense of purpose. The sooner you accept that conflict is inevitable, the better you can prepare to work through it.

How Conflict Reveals Who You Really Are

Two of the silliest assumptions you can believe are that everyone else is like you and that no one else is like you.

We are not meant to live in boxes. We're each unique, yet cut from the same body-and-spirit cloth. None of us is completely similar to another, but we're not altogether unlike each other, either.

Part of what makes you uniquely human is the story of how you've dealt with conflict. You can't wrestle depression, cancer, or unemployment without changing something in the construct of your identity—or at least you shouldn't be able to. The way you deal with resistance puts you on the fast track to developing character and integrity.

In light of that, the American Dream becomes problematic because it tends to rob people of the opportunity for greater adventure, for falling down into the trenches of life where battles of the soul are fought. The American Dream's call to comfort, security, and predictability is rooted in self-centeredness. Unaddressed, it leaves only a shell of a person after a long life of comfort and few disruptions, a man or woman who has existed but barely ever lived. Anne Lamott put it like this: "If we stay where we are, where we're stuck, where we're comfortable and safe, we die there...When nothing new can get in, that's death."[119]

Conflict not only reveals one's identity—it also refines it. You can tell a lot by the way someone encounters resistance; it allows the authentic personality to emerge. In the intensity of conflict, you shed what you don't need. You get focused on the bare essentials about who you are and what you must do. Conflict is an opportunity to gain clarity.

This works its way into our relationship with God and with others. You can't wrestle with God over your dreams and your fears without walking away a little bewildered and sore, but grateful for what you've learned. The fights we have with our spouses, best friends, families, and coworkers shape us and reveal who we are far more effectively than our comfortable, predictable routines.

In the end, God's not even opposed to comfort; it's just that he invites us to find our comfort, not in shallow things like homes, financial prosperity, and American Dreams, but in knowing and living in connection with him.

The whole story of God and humanity revolves around this: he is with us through every conflict. Our job is not to resolve the conflict, but to walk with him through it, so we can help others navigate their conflicts, too.[120]

44

Hoping for Home

*"The world is a book, and those who
do not travel read only one page."*

AUGUSTINE OF HIPPO

Whenever returning from a week of travel, I feel a sort of depression sneaking up on me. It usually starts on the plane one or two connections before arriving back in my city. The wistful sense of bittersweet memories permeates my gut, and it creeps up into my mind by the time I've landed at home.

This post-event mood swing has emerged at various times over the past six or seven years. I felt the depression every August during college. When I traveled with the small team of college students each summer, I grew emotionally and spiritually, and in my love of travel. Ten weeks on the road was tiring, but not draining. It fed my hunger for adventure. New states and cities and skylines quickly became new friends to my heart and my camera lens.

I felt at home on the road. Mile markers and hotel rooms weren't so bad when travel was such an inspiration. Thirty thousand feet in the air became my favorite place to reflect, to dream, and to regain perspective. Upon my return from these traveling summers, I lived with my parents until classes started again in the fall. Before a week passed, I sank into boredom and apathy. The transition to quiet home life was a jarring juxtaposition.

Long-distance relationships and airport goodbyes are the worst, too. I'm sure you've felt that sting of farewell. Apprehensive goodbyes tear us up inside, even if we know we'll see the same person again.

I cried like a baby the day I returned from an eventful two-week adventure. The first week, it was the student mission trip in Atlanta, then I spent a few days in Salt Lake City to be in Nate and Robyn's wedding. Kati held me as I wept on the couch when it was all over. It's clearest in moments like this that I'm better with someone by my side. Her welcoming arms and grateful smile help me readjust to life in our city. The people I love are the greatest benefits to coming home.

Still, the emotions linger. For days, I recount the trip and grow more remorseful that it's now a memory, locked in the past. An adventure is over, and I grieve the loss of the experience.

I've heard it said "a change of place plus a change of pace equals a change of perspective."[121]

We're made for more than brief adventures. We sense the pull to be part of a bigger story and experience roads and cities and worlds foreign to us, yet strangely welcoming. I don't know what you think about the kingdom of heaven, but I get the sense it will be like finding the home we've all been searching for and being welcomed into it.[122]

Travelers

There's a part of the Bible that says we're all travelers in a way, in one place but looking forward to something else. Peter wrote:

> Dear friends, I warn you as temporary residents and foreigners to keep away from worldly desires that wage war against your very souls. Be careful to live properly among your unbelieving neighbors. Then

even if they accuse you of doing wrong, they will see
your honorable behavior, and they will give honor to
God when he judges the world.[123]

Despite what religions and science say, I don't know whether to believe humans have been on the earth for ages or only recently in the history of the universe. I'm not sure if the planet is thousands of years old or billions, or even if it matters that much. But I know we don't own the place, all this soil and rock and vegetation. We won't be here forever in the same way we're here now. It's as if we don't belong here because we're made for another place, or rather, we're changing and we'll experience something entirely new, yet fitting—birthed through the here and now, but going far beyond it.

When the original audience heard those words about being temporary residents and foreigners, they would have recalled Israel's life in exile, being taken away from their homeland and held captive in the Babylonian empire. They would have remembered the prophet Jeremiah's words about living faithfully in a pagan culture, and the story of Daniel and his friends as examples of integrity in the midst of hostility.[124] Peter described the people of God as "temporary residents and foreigners," and Paul explained "our citizenship in heaven," highlighting how our allegiance belongs to something else, but we live in this current reality.[125] The theme of exile is a common one in the Bible, that depicts life on earth until the kingdom of God arrives in fullness and wrongs are made right. To live in the way of Jesus is to cling to our God-given identity and practice while dwelling in a drastically different culture.

I think I understand what the author meant when he said "worldly desires that wage war against your very souls." I've seen some terrible things take over someone's life, and I've heard even worse. Most of us haven't experienced the worst evils firsthand, like kids in Sudan who were brainwashed to be soldiers for the pillaging bandits who killed their parents.

Or like innocent Christians, Muslims, and Yazidis forced from their homes in Syria and Iraq by the violent extremists of ISIS. For the most part, we have clean, running water in our homes and can easily access food by driving to the grocery store instead of walking miles through a dry, barren landscape. Few people I know have lived on the streets, teetered on the brink of starvation, or had to bail someone out of jail.

My life's pretty good by comparison—but that's the catch. The comparison game turns ugly. It puts a negative filter on even good things when I care more about my status at the expense of someone else's. How do I match up to my neighbor's charisma, popularity, and career success? How much higher is the median income in our country compared to that country? How many times have my peers upgraded to the newest smartphone or car while I'm still using the previous model?

"Worldly desires" get mixed into the psyche of people who think they're doing the right thing. In the 2012 movie *Chronicle*, three teenage boys get superpowers from some mysterious radiation, and they spend the movie experimenting with their newfound abilities. At one point, the protagonist feels helpless to aid his dying mother, but realizes he can use his powers to rob a gas station to pay for her medication. It snowballs into a whole mess of situations in which he can't help but exercise his abilities to serve his own wishes. He ultimately faces the choice to surrender and get help from his friends or keep destroying people's lives just because he can. Evil seems to creep in like that, convincing us to do a little more, get a little further. Left unchecked, our own desires turn us into the monsters we resent.

In the 1 Peter 2 passage, Peter directs attention to the other-worldliness we're made for, but still doesn't excuse our behavior in the here and now. Even the way we treat those who may not share our beliefs or values is important enough for God to remind us about it.

According to Peter, God will one day judge the world and call to account the forces that work against the flourishing of humanity. Wrongs will be set right, and justice will prevail over all that holds it back today. God designed us all with a sense of honor, dignity, and kindness to share, and something is beautifully fulfilled when human behavior reflects God's intentions.

As we journey though life, like foreigners searching for a lasting sense of home, God whispers through the madness that wages war against our souls. He whispers honor and belonging and hope to us amidst the tension, beckoning us to find our place in a home beyond the world in its current state, but reminding us to stay engaged in the present. He doesn't want us to shirk responsibility, or become *so heavenly minded that we are no earthly good*, as the saying goes.[126] God's given us a path to walk and fellow travelers to keep our pace steady and our vision clear. There is much to do in the meantime. We travel in the here and now, hoping to find home and catching glimpses of it along the way.

Maybe that's why travel is such a powerful thing: we're always looking for places we feel we belong.

45

A Taste of Heaven

"The present world is also designed for something which has not yet happened. It is like a violin waiting to be played: beautiful to look at, graceful to hold—and yet if you'd never heard one in the hands of a musician, you wouldn't believe the new dimensions of beauty yet to be revealed."

N. T. WRIGHT

Brian invited a bunch of us from across the country to join him in South Carolina. He would be marrying Danielle one April afternoon, and we wouldn't miss it for anything. It was a reconvening of our closest circle of friends: the four of us from Minnesota, young men who had grown so close through music and asking big questions of life and of God. Seth, Nate, and Robyn still lived in Minnesota, so they drove to South Carolina. Kati and I flew from Oregon. Brian and Danielle awaited our arrival to Greenville the week of their wedding. Though we had moved to different cities spanning the nation, we kept in touch and eagerly planned our trips to celebrate the big day.

Flying coast to coast took all day, so Kati and I wearily stumbled off the plane in Charlotte and picked up a rental car after midnight local time. Exhausted from working overnight and two layovers, she fell asleep in the passenger seat. I drove across the border into South Carolina with my favorite satellite radio station on the stereo, my spirit rising with the melodies in anticipation of reuniting with the dearest friends a person could ask for.

It was around two in the morning when we pulled into the dark parking lot of Brian's apartment complex, and after a moment his figure emerged from the porch and welcomed us with big hugs. Kati and I rolled our luggage into the apartment, where Nate and Robyn sat on the couch and Seth lay nearly asleep on a mattress on the floor. After a few minutes of eager greetings, we said goodnight and Brian showed us to a spare bedroom.

I lay in bed, listening to Kati's steady breathing beside me while staring at the ceiling fan in the dark. Maybe it was because my body considered it not even midnight Pacific Time, but I couldn't fall asleep. My mind raced with the schedule of the next few days, the short but sweet time I would share with my closest companions before we again dispersed to different corners of the country.

It was only three years ago in this same city—Greenville, South Carolina—that the four of us wondered at the miracle of God intertwining our stories. Our variable lives once again brought us together to celebrate, to reminisce, and to dream up what else the future would hold. And we knew our brotherhood was far from over.

I finally drifted off to sleep—grateful for my friends, for a chance to celebrate the start of something new with Brian and Danielle, for my wife next to me, and for the adventures my life offered because of the relationships God provided.

Together

The wedding was beautiful, held at a plantation set on a hill overlooking the Blue Ridge Mountains—the foothills of the mighty Appalachians. South Carolina put on her best spring blue sky and sunshine, complete with a cool breeze (which was most appreciated by those of us wearing three-piece suits). Brian grinned ear to ear with tears streaming down his face when his bride appeared in white. With a beaming smile and blonde hair dancing in the wind, Danielle grew more radiant with each step toward the white pergola standing before the audience.

After we sent off the bride and groom with a car full of balloons, streamers, and joyful farewells, the reception came to a timely conclusion. Remaining cake was packed away, tables were removed, and rental tuxes were tucked into garment bags. It felt good to send off Brian and Danielle, all married and happy, like we played a part in accomplishing the destiny they were bound for.

There's a magical feeling when you complete a task with people you love. Through meeting a need or surpassing a challenge together, your relationship sprouts durable roots. These roots go deeper than acquaintances you merely hang around or share a few sedentary conversations with. Adventure begs for company. When we get off the couch and go experience something together, we are better for it. Whenever I see an amazing sunset, God's pastel strokes across the wide skies, I send a picture of it to my family or call for my wife to watch it with me.

I thought about this as we drove away from the picturesque plantation. The wedding party and our spouses decided to spend the evening in downtown Greenville, soaking in the city together for the last time.

We walked through Falls Park on the river, in the middle of a lively downtown, filled with romancing couples and picnicking families enjoying the spring evening. The expansive Liberty Bridge was all lit up under the fading skies, and our attention turned to our appetites.

Sharing the Table

We submitted a reservation at a restaurant, and the eight of us packed into the back room with a full-length window to the streets of Greenville. Smiles emerged on each face around the table: Seth, Nate and Robyn, Jordan, Jacob and Jessica, Kati, and myself. It was the final meal we would all share before going our separate ways.

Like a close-knit family, we passed plates around the table to share tastes. There we were—a group of friends brought together by love for a couple we held dear, and in doing so, we grew nearer to each other.

Sitting back from the table, I surveyed the joyful faces accompanying the earnest questions and personal stories floating around like the smoke lazily swirling above our heads. Here was a profound moment, and Jessica spoke what we each sensed:

"It seems like this is what heaven or the kingdom of God is like—just being with people we love, sitting around a table, eating great food, talking about meaningful things and how Jesus has worked in our lives."

I knew it was true when she said it. The divine became observable, less nebulous and more tangible. It's just like God to usher us into that picture of what he's designed for humanity: the peace and joy of connection between people.

There is a world we cannot yet see clearly, but dim fragments make their way into our lives on occasion. At the core of profound joy is the spark of the divine, a hint of things to come— God whispering, *This is how things should be: bound together in love, celebrating what is good and right and true. Even now, as you live out your story, you can connect the things of heaven with the things of earth.*

Heaven Meets Earth

The Bible talks a lot about heaven and hell and earth and the kingdom of God. You could read plenty of other books that explain it far better than I can[127], but this is something that reshaped my view of the world beyond our present.

I used to think heaven was a place with fluffy clouds where

fairy-like angels floated about, playing harps and the like. Surely there were great treasures and streets of gold all encompassed by huge gates to keep out bad people, and lots of choirs angelically singing everyone's favorite Sunday school songs. Of course, God—his enormous white beard, his grandfatherly characteristics—sat on the throne, and people could wander in and pay their respects before returning to their individual mansions for a pleasant, glowing eternal life.

A while ago, I realized this image of heaven is merely a glorified vacation resort in the sky—a twisted parody of various passages in the Bible. Nate is a pastor, and when he preaches, he calls this the "disembodied soul evacuation when you die" perspective, which is pretty catchy. Life on earth is useless and terrible, so why try to enjoy it? Just live a good-enough life until your soul can leave your wretched body on this rotten planet and escape to the sanitized bliss and safety of heaven.

I don't think that's how Jesus intended for us to see life after death, or life on earth.

When he talked about the kingdom of heaven, Jesus spoke about people being fully united with God, making all things right, and restoring relationships between people and himself. The kingdom of God is a place where the sick are healed, the lowly are regarded, and the outcasts are welcome.[128] When God receives people into his heavenly kingdom, they don't lack anymore. There's nothing to need when we meet our maker. The desire for meaning and belonging is fulfilled. But somehow, we won't experience that higher level of unbridled connection with God until something big changes.

Throughout his life on earth, Jesus insisted on the intersection—not the separation—of heaven and earth.[129] We can experience the presence of our creator both here and now, and in the age to come. Glimpses of the kingdom of God can show up on earth and the world can be changed by its power, even before it arrives in full.

One church leader, who was persecuted and arrested in 1950s Communist China, wrote:

The kingdom of God is at once present and to come. As to time, it lies ahead of us; as to experience, it is ours today. God intends us to enjoy foretastes here and now of the powers of the future age.[130]

That didn't just change his outlook; that changed his actions. In the kingdom of heaven, there is no injustice and no pain. Humanity is connected in unbroken community, and God reigns as a good and noble king who makes all things new.[131] Our task is to bring these heavenly qualities to earth so people can experience the goodness of God for themselves, here and now.

Knowing God is what we're made for. It's the satisfaction we seek when we're navigating life, looking for something lasting to make us finally fulfilled. God is where healing begins, both personal and cosmic. A path of awakening and belonging await; as we turn away from our harmful foolishness and sin, we can turn toward Jesus, the tangible grace of God.

Repentance is what gets us there—when we change our mind and admit we can't figure it out on our own. By dealing with our sins, both individual and systemic, he reconciled us with God and made peace.[132] His resurrection proved death is not the end, and all things can be made new.[133] That is the gospel, and it is good news for all of us.

Jesus is the one who forever connected heaven and earth, giving us second and third and thousandth chances to experience God's sustaining love despite our failures. We wander from the path of meaningful living, but Jesus stands with open arms. When we stray, he is ready to lead us back to quiet revelations and community with others on the same challenging journey. We don't have to live in shame or fear anymore. We don't have to prove we're good enough to belong. Jesus already brought us into God's family and the mission to bring more good, kindness, and justice to the world.

It's not just about a journey or a destination. The divine is breaking into the world in beautiful ways, and we can welcome it together.

46

Adventures Worth Sharing

*"The real voyage of discovery consists not in seeking
new landscapes, but in having new eyes."*

MARCEL PROUST

One day in the fall, Kati and I buckled into the car and picked up our niece and our friend Chris. Just outside our city in Oregon, scores of dirt roads and trails lead through fields and forests and up into the Cascade Mountains.

We drove past the park entrance and successive parking lots, past the picnic tables and volleyball courts, to the edge of the woods that backed up against the Rogue River. A meandering footpath led us near blackberry bushes taller than we could reach, over a gravel road used by grouse hunters, and finally into a few clearings near shallow turns of the Rogue.

The deep green leaves were beginning to turn into the autumn versions of themselves, fresh and flexible forsaken into the weathered, brittle collections crushed into the ground. The ripe blackberries tasted bitter and wild, but offered a welcome sign of life amidst the flora shutting down before winter winds threatened our valley.

It wasn't long before our blonde, uninhibited three-year-old niece became infatuated with a new focus at every turn of the path. First, the steep river shoreline; second, the tall grassy fields; next, the tantalizing blackberries; and then the stones perched at the river's bend.

Chris looked like a woodsman who belonged there, with a couple days' stubble hinting at a beard, his flannel shirt, and a stern gaze that turned into a satisfied smile to let you know he was glad to be outdoors. He tossed a few smooth stones into the river's current. Kati and I robotically followed his precedent. It wasn't long before our niece insisted on joining our activity, choosing larger and larger rocks as she went. Despite our suggestions to find more manageably sized stones, she eyed the endless rock supply on the riverbank in search of the largest inanimate victim to promptly launch into the flowing waters.

Stepping back to watch the scene that day reminded me of my childhood, and maybe it reminds you of yours. Our niece experienced some of the first changes of fall that year. Her eyes were wide with wonder at every turn. Colorful leaves, berry bushes, and throwing rocks in the river became new again.

What Children Have

Through my niece's experience, Kati and Chris and I grew nostalgic about our childhoods. Stepping back into the mind of a child provided us the lens of amazement—of a grander, more mysterious world yet unknown to us. A three-year-old doesn't worry about tomorrow, bills to pay, or a career plan. She doesn't lament when told there's only one car in the garage, or if there's even a garage in the first place.

Children have something still embedded within them that most adults have long since lost: wonder. They dare to dream, to be inspired, to explore the muddy shoreline and throw rocks in the water to make the biggest splash. Birds' nests and fallen trees in the forest transform into an exciting world—a limitless playground for young ones. Where adults see normalcy and routine, a child sees possibility, mystery, and fun. "No one is ever satisfied where he is...Only the children know what they're looking for."[134]

Too often, I'm lost in the routine of adulthood with bills, work, car maintenance, and stressing over relationships I can't control. We need to live in less rigidity and more whimsy and adventure, forsaking numbness toward what we've come to know as real life.

Our lives cultivate more meaning when we seek adventure and indulge in childlike amazement rather than disinterestedly view the cold, real world. Swiss psychiatrist and adventure balloonist Bertrand Piccard said, "The pioneering spirit is less about thinking up new ideas, as ridding ourselves of dogmas and habits that hold us captive in old ways of thinking and acting."[135]

Perhaps the key to childlike wonder is staying open-minded, not succumbing to the status quo. I'm not saying we throw all caution, planning, and responsibility to the wind, but that there's room for both structure and spontaneity. The conflict between the two isn't a problem to solve, but a tension to manage. Responsibility isn't the opposite of adventure; complacency is. Becoming stagnant and satisfied with the status quo is what kills our wonder.

It's the same way with people. As we surround ourselves with friends or acquaintances, we experience greater familiarity and then similarity. We become who we spend time with.

That's one of the reasons I schedule time with those who have a strong sense of adventure, passion, and creativity. Do you know how refreshing it is to be around people who experience a new environment or new idea or new activity, and transfer that passion to those around them? They stir something bold in us, gently urging us to inject more excitement into our lives. At first, it may be a little dizzying with all their new-found zeal, but that's usually what's missing from those of us who've experienced years of doubt and pain that morph into weary jadedness.

Being an adult feels like the pits sometimes: it can sap the energy and enthusiasm right out of us. But those who haven't been crushed by years of living are full of courage and passion. They live with purpose, admitting both the joys and the sorrows. Youthful optimism isn't irrelevant just because we've gotten older. It must be a state of mind, because my Aunt Margie is 96 and she still goes dancing every Sunday night.

Better for It

Kati and I met Jordan the week of Brian and Danielle's wedding in South Carolina. The day after the wedding, Jordan didn't have to fly back to Washington State until later that afternoon, so we invited him to join us for a hike. We ate brunch at Waffle House—because that's what you do when you visit the South— before we drove north out of Greenville in search of adventure. Jordan eagerly ate hash browns and toast at Waffle House, carrying on conversation like it was his job. He knew how to ask really good questions to learn about people. He listened like he genuinely cared about what we told him.

We drove to a state park called Table Rock, a huge rock formation at the foothills of the Blue Ridge Mountains. The three of us set out just after noon, grateful for a chance to enjoy the sunny Southern weather. Throughout our couple miles of hiking, Jordan told us about his wife and how they met, how their families interact, and what it's like to live in a town largely populated by college students.

Kati and I were already excited to be there, to explore a new place in a different state. Having Jordan along for the experience boosted our excitement even more. Jordan's affirming presence radiated from behind his beard, black-rimmed glasses, and baseball cap. The conversation during the hike refreshed us more than the physical exercise did.

That's what you see when you surround yourself with people motivated to live beyond themselves: passion is contagious.

When your life is peppered with people who are different from you, yet you allow their perspective to influence you, both of you walk away better for it. You each have a piece of the other, a small landmark of the way he or she is figuring out life. It can impact you more than your own ideas do, if you let it.

I like how Anne Lamott explained the power of shared life:

> Most humbling of all is to comprehend the lifesaving gift that your pit crew of people has been for you, and all the experiences you have shared, the journeys together, the collaborations, births and deaths, divorces, rehab, and vacations, the solidarity you have shown one another. Every so often you realize that without all of them, your life would be barren and pathetic. It would be Death of a Salesman, though with e-mail and texting.[136]

These days, I try to look at people as adventures, too. It's unquestionably easier to sit on the couch with a good book or to merely send a text message when I need something from someone, but it's a different kind of reward to step into the world of another person for a while.

Being in someone else's world takes us out of our comfortable routine and helps us see in a new way. We've all heard the old adage, "You'll never understand someone until you walk a mile in his shoes." We learn what someone thinks when we walk a mile in his shoes, but we learn what someone lives for when we walk even further together.

It matters when we look at something from another's perspective and even more when we continue a conversation—each sharing, listening, and connecting with the world around us. That's what adventure is: engaging a new experience worth sharing with someone else. And like my friend Christian says, adventures don't start until you're off the beaten path.

47

An Evening with the Elderly

*"Two things that make the world a poorer place: young people
who ask no questions and old people who offer no wisdom."*

TYLER BRAUN

When fall comes to Southern Oregon, the dry summer heat
stubbornly hangs on as long as it can, then reluctantly gives
way to cool rains and fog. One of those overcast days in October, I spent a late afternoon with a few dozen senior citizens in
my church. I was invited to a dinner hosted by the group, along
with Nick and his wife, Katie. We sat around a table with people who had lived through entire generations before we were
born or our parents had even met.

I grabbed my acoustic guitar after dessert was served, and
Katie and I sang a few songs for everyone. I chose a couple old
hymns the audience remembered and a more current song so
they could get a taste of something different. Nick took the
microphone and spoke about the church's community of eigh-
teen- to twentysomethings, the group that welcomed me so
kindly when I had just moved there from Minnesota two short
years ago.

Nick shared how he started the group, how we talk about the
Bible and learn to align our lives around God with each other's support. He explained how many in the Millennial generation have been burned by previous experiences with organized

religion, so there are often discrepancies in the way we perceive church, culture, faith, and Jesus. Those are the kinds of things the community of young adults discussed as we studied the Bible and built relationships. This explanation gave the elderly insight into what young adults of our church were involved in. Perhaps it was one of the only times they really heard what young people exploring faith do in a place like Southern Oregon.

Nick went on to tell parts of his story, starting with how his unmarried mother, between drug relapses and against the expectations of friends and family, decided not to have an abortion or give him up for adoption. The elderly audience listened with rapt curiosity.

Nick has a beautiful story. He elaborated on his childhood in Southern California, amidst gang attacks on neighbors, being raised by his grandparents, and carrying guilt-ridden anger into his adulthood. Inner turmoil and questioning his self-worth nearly sabotaged his marriage before it even started. Growing up without a father led to doubt that he could raise his two daughters and his son on the way.

Frequently, Nick reflects on the miracle that he's still alive and in the middle of such an abundant life. He's completely in love with his wife and raises his children with such consistent kindness that it's hard to believe he came from a history of drug abuse, bitterness, and unstable parenting. These marks are common in modern families, yet like Nick experienced so much change for the better, others who face the same cycle of generational challenges can change, too.

Nick would be the first to tell you God deserves the credit for transforming his life. He knows he's been rescued from great darkness and he lives with renewed purpose because of it. Nick also praises his grandparents, who raised him like he was their own son while his mother was absent and there was no father to speak of. Especially after the death of his grandmother, Nick cherished the memories of growing up under the care and provision of his grandparents during the turbulent years of his youth.

Legacy

Looking around a room full of thick glasses, walking canes, and gray hair (or no hair at all), it made me thankful like Nick is thankful. I became grateful for the efforts of people who had done so much to prepare the way for new waves of people to grow up and to thrive in a community. Over the years, these men and women led families, prepared countless dinners, and drove kids to Little League. They pinched pennies during economic depressions and hosted family reunions. Many have told stories of their lives and passed the baton of faith to the next generation.

It would be arrogant of us younger generations to claim we haven't been empowered by those who've gone before us. I like that the elderly attendees of that church called themselves the Legacy group. It speaks to what they value; they want to leave a legacy of following Jesus and contributing to the kingdom of God with all the resources and energy they can muster. In a way, it's already fulfilled. The most visible legacy left by older people is us—you and me. We occupy a position with loads of potential. A vast horizon sprawls before us, beckoning our best efforts, our wisest risks, and our full hearts.

Nick says that because his grandparents sacrificed so much to raise him well, he was propelled toward an abundant life. God worked through his grandparents to show love for a messed-up problem child who went on to become a pastor who teaches and loves messed-up problem people.

Grandparents, along with parents, teachers, supervisors, professors, and mentors, have built a bridge for us into the future, into better things, and hopefully into deeper faith. This isn't about passing on the American Dream, financial prosperity, or just a good life. A good life means nothing apart from the purpose God gives it. Jesus is direct about what he wants for us: that we live in fullness, healed from our blindness and freed from our brokenness.[137] God uses the legacy of previous generations to continue the story he's writing with each of us today.

It makes me want to call and thank everyone who's contributed to my story, and everyone who's invited me into theirs. It's invigorating to remember where we've come from and the people who helped make our lives what they are. As poet Wendell Berry said, "If you don't know where you're from, you'll have a hard time saying where you're going."[138]

Our variable lives make more sense in the context of the expansive narrative that's been playing out for millennia. We contribute our best when we find our place in the story.

48

Don't Give Up

"If you're not dead, you're not done. Your best days are before you."
CRAIG GROESCHEL

Kati worked at one of the hospitals in Southern Oregon. One day, an author was in for a checkup. She told him she was married to an aspiring writer, and asked what advice I should consider as I write more and more. Without a moment's hesitation, the author simply said, "Don't give up." When Kati told me, I wanted to drive to the hospital, shake the man's hand, and listen to his story.

There have been scores of times when giving up was clearly the easiest—and perhaps sanest—thing to do. When I first got excited about writing, posting blog entries on the Internet felt as useful as shouting down a thunderstorm: you might see something cool happen, but not from anything you've contributed. When I began writing a book, months bled into years. Working a fulltime job, volunteer roles, hobbies, and trying to be a good friend kept my writing from gaining any real momentum. The temptation to call it quits was ever-present. Barely anyone would have known, much less cared, if I had pushed the ambition out of sight. To most of the world, except for a few of my family members, friends, and a dozen blog readers, the book didn't even exist. I could have proved its irrelevance to myself, but it felt like I wasn't allowed to give up. Were it not for an unforgiving urge to keep writing the pages you see now, it would not exist today.

Anyone who has ever birthed something out of nothing knows the tenacity it requires. It's a miracle God didn't set humanity aside the moment chaos erupted. Every day, we grapple with the decision to give up or press on. Maybe it's your job or a relationship, or perhaps you're even at a place in your life where you can't see the point anymore. Sometimes the only reason we continue is because we don't want to let down the people surrounding us. Quitting is always an option, but it is never the only one.

Perspective

One of the most powerful parts of the Bible is in a letter written during the first century AD. Paul wrote to a group in the Greek city of Corinth. In the letter, he explained the danger they faced within a largely pagan and hostile culture, and the targeted persecution they had endured wasn't all that was going on.

Paul was a pretty audacious guy. He told the Corinthians that living in the face of death actually resulted in a sort of ongoing life. Paul was so bold because Jesus, whose power was far greater than the oppressive Roman Empire, had transformed him. He didn't fear physical harm or death because he had experienced something superior to violent threats and military might. Even under the jurisdiction of the strongest world power of that time, Paul urged the Corinthians not to let fear guide them:

> All this is for your benefit, so that the grace that is reaching more and more people may cause thanksgiving to overflow to the glory of God. Therefore we do not lose heart. Though outwardly we are wasting away, yet inwardly we are being renewed day by day.

For our light and momentary troubles are achieving for us an eternal glory that far outweighs them all. So we fix our eyes not on what is seen, but on what is unseen, since what is seen is temporary, but what is unseen is eternal.[139]

How could Paul say with any assurance that their current danger was not a major problem, but was only temporary? From a human perspective, it looked like the beginning of the end: followers of Jesus martyred and the movement of Christianity stamped out.

If Paul were a filmmaker, he'd pull back the frame, up and up to the 30,000-foot view to show what else was happening. The church in Corinth faced brutal conflict, yes—but that conflict was not the deepest reality of their lives.

No one reading the letter from Paul doubted his credibility when he stated their bodies were dying. To be alive is to slowly return that life to the dust where it began. The crazy thing about what Paul wrote was that, during the gradual devolution and threats against their bodies, they still saw glimpses of healing and their spirits being renewed. In that moment, their physical condition and spiritual condition were not limited by each other; they worked together to produce a more resilient, beautiful reality. Things seemed bleak, but those followers of Jesus needed to hear that "death is something empires worry about...not something resurrection people worry about."[140]

Current situations can never define what's timelessly significant. The resistance they faced did not dictate the potential they carried. Like a pure diamond displayed over black velvet, the backdrop of conflict allowed what was most valuable to shine through.

Finding Your Place

God offers fresh perspective. He beckons us to climb up to that

30,000-foot view and sit there on the edge with him, looking down and reflecting on it all. Within the context of a larger story, we each find our meaning and our place. We're not merely cogs in the wheel of society, but valuable individuals with something uniquely me and you to contribute. A person with connections, passions, and skills isn't just fulfilling tasks. You are a living contributor in the ever-evolving story of humanity. As one poet put it, "You owe it to all of us to get on with what you're good at."[141]

The way we live widens or fills the gaps in the story. It's the difference between a movie ridden with plot holes or an award-winning masterpiece. Giving up would mean others around us would miss out on something, too; they'd miss out on someone who influences them and adds contour, depth, and richness to all these stories woven together.

Don't give up. Don't leave others lacking the role you play in their story. Don't drift away when things get tough; lean in. I am still learning what this means, to advance someone else's story, so perhaps we can learn it together. Our refusal to give up will make an impact in the bigger narrative—maybe not at first or even for a while, but the slow, steady work of living fully and being present in our work and relationships can change you and change others.

One of my friends is an actor, and I love this line from a play he performed: "There's something way down deep that's eternal about every human being."[142]

Something tangibly temporary yet eternally significant is happening in you and in me, even when we can't see it. Eventually, the present will fade into the past and glory will be more real than any of the conflicts we endured, and we will know it was worth it to not give up.

49

The End of the Road

"What you leave behind is not what is engraved in stone monuments, but what is woven into the lives of others."

PERICLES

The Return of the King just doesn't want to end. At the end of the epic tale where good triumphs over evil in a final battle, the Hobbits return to the Shire, and Frodo and Bilbo sail away from Middle-earth. When the film fades to black, the music plays for a moment and then fades up into another scene. Then a new story kicks into gear, following Samwise's resumed life.

The first time I watched it, I felt like the film producers were toying with my emotions. I couldn't land on any closure with all those different possible ending points. Don't get me wrong: I've loved *The Lord of the Rings* since I first read the books during high school. But thinking about those films years after viewing them, I realized something about the nature of stories.

At the end of every series of movies, there's a glimmer of more. More often than not, at the end of a trilogy, another story begins. Even in a stand-alone film, when all is said and done and the couple is reunited to marry or the bad guys are defeated, one final snapshot plays before the screen goes dark. As an audience, we expect the story to finish, the credits to roll, and closure to set in. But at the end of all things, there is another thing.

The Cycle

I wrote much of this book sitting at the kitchen table, staring out the window to summer sunsets in Southern Oregon. Pacific Northwest sunsets are some of the finest. The dramatic clouds and vibrant hues rival any land's beauty. So many of those evenings, the clouds performed their chameleon act, scattered across a pale blue backdrop with their purple darks and orange fringes turned pink. Clouds seem to move faster toward sunset, as if they know it's time to hurry to the horizon for a good night's rest.

I've heard perspective grows much clearer at the end of one's life. I hope the clarity we gain at the end of our road is a sharp image of the ways we've grasped our variable opportunities with passion and tenacity. To face the last moments of this existence with only regrets seems the most terrible realization of a lifetime, because it's the culmination of a life that was less than it could have been.

"God made man because he loves stories," Elie Wiesel told us.[143] I've gone through moments and seasons of regretful living, those times I know I could've done better. To avoid regret, we must live in such a way now that we will someday relish what was instead of wondering what could have been.

Regardless of our performance, the only consolation in a life speckled with regret is to rest in a divine promise. Promises are the language of God. He always invites us to trust him and trust he will provide down the road.

God emerges in the most unlikely places when we look back on our stories. His presence is at the core of any promise he's ever made. When we say yes to him, we're changed for the better, and life is the process of experiencing those changes.

Your story is far from over. God is still shaping your body, mind, and spirit with the molds of grace and truth. Your story has many chapters yet to write. There are still conflicts to overcome, people to journey with, and new places to discover. And when you think it's over, wait a little longer or chase a lead, and a new chapter will surface right before you.

Coming to the end of something takes us right back to the beginning.

I imagine when I'm old and retiring from my last job, I'll reminisce on the first job I held. I'll think about how it all started, my life as a contributing adult, and I'll wonder if I did anything worth leaving behind. The end of one thing is always connected to the start of another.

Stories lead to more stories, like love causes more love, just as hope in one person multiplies to more people. There's no finish line in the human story. It's all an ongoing cycle: life and death, stories and their telling, humanity, and our search for meaning.

In the end, all our stories will fit with all the other stories in the world to form an astounding, overarching narrative. It's bigger than we can see, far too complex and nuanced to make sense from our perspectives contained within space and time. The complexity feels overwhelming yet familiar, like it's where we belong.

Scenes

In a flash, I see the moments of my childhood, when I needed direction and correction, and how God provided the nurturing environment I needed to see the beautiful fragility of people. I see my childhood self sledding in Minnesota's winter white, making tracks in the snow because I wanted to get somewhere further than I'd been and feel exhilaration that I hadn't yet felt. I see the frustration of teenage loves gone wrong and how it gave me a realistic view of the risky nature of relationships. I have witnessed how an adamant introvert can embrace more meaningful time with people because they are worth it, while still nurturing inner thoughts and the curiosity of questions in solitude—a sustainable cycle that feeds the individual and the community.

The scenes keep scrolling. I see the summer-long road trips and the towering mountains that magnetically attracted me, and how my sense for adventure was cultivated in such a way that I grew ready for more than I was living. That readiness urged me to pack up a car full of belongings and move away from my family, friends, and all I'd ever known to work and live in a foreign place. And I see how that place became not just a valley I lived in, surrounded by Oregon's mountains, but a symbol for my awakening love of the outdoors and the transformation I would experience when I gathered the courage to fully immerse myself in a new chapter of life. No turning back; no holding on to what was.

I see how God, in his masterful timing and kindness, crossed my path with Kati's and set us on a journey of learning the ways in which we're right for each other and how we make each other better. I see now it's all building toward something: another phase in which I'm learning we each have to make a few sacrifices in order to live a better story.

If we forgo small comforts, we can do more things worth remembering. I'm learning, maybe like you've already learned, how to value people different from myself and live with no regard for what I'm supposed to do so I can do what's best.

I see myself in a room with Brian, Seth, Nate, and the scores of dear friends who contributed to the best moments in my life—the people who helped make me who I am. I know there will be more nights of celebration and memories, tense conversations and uncomfortable challenges, but there will also be nights of dreaming up the future of our lives together. I see that more friends will become brothers and sisters to me, and I to them. And I know that no single city will be my home forever, because so many different places have changed me in the ways

I needed.

There is tremendous beauty in the complexity life offers. The way I've adapted through the changes, conflicts, and relationships of my life are unforgettable, undeniable. Those are the things that give us clarity and confidence in a world of choices.

In my mind's eye, the camera pulls back and back, away from our personal stories, our communities, and the stories in our cities and nations, now with the whole world in view. And the camera pulls back even further, outside the solar system, away from the tiny galaxy among galaxies. And I imagine God sitting at his desk, putting the finishing touches on a page, and we realize he's been working on and in our story all along.

At the end of your journey—even now, in this moment—I hope you can look back at a purposeful and passionate story you've lived. I hope you can see how you've become the best version of yourself through the changes you've experienced, the conflict you've endured, and the relationships you've embraced. And I hope you gain clarity and confidence throughout your own variable life.

50

Epilogue

Early one November morning, the mountains of Southern Oregon faded in the rearview mirror as Kati and I left town. We had given away furniture, clothing, and accessories we no longer needed, and had maybe never needed in the first place. We'd shipped one of the cars and our minimized belongings. It had been freeing to release things we'd owned but that didn't really belong with us.

We didn't need what we'd thought we did. That was the perspective we adopted gradually, because we'd entered into a new revelation on our path—one we had never predicted.

In our new life, in a distant place, we would build something new. It would not be a completely new life, built from nothing. It could not be a blank-slate beginning, but we did not want it to be. We wanted a continuation of the story we were living, the same story in which our friends and our families had played immense parts and would continue to.

That November morning, an astonishing sunrise sent its first rays into the sky as we gave Kati's family a final farewell. It wasn't long before our view of the morning sun washed out in the cold fog covering the two-lane highway out of town.

We headed east.

What we left behind faded from view, and a whole unknown future was ahead of us. The thick fog enveloped our small SUV packed with belongings. The land sprawled out like it always had, inviting adventurous hearts to seek out unfamiliar places.

Forward

Life is often like that, guiding us to a point of decision. We must stay and maintain the status quo we've become so comfortably accustomed to, or we must pack up and move on. The journey is not guaranteed to be safe, to go according to plan, or to be clear at every turn. But we must keep going, into the fog, into the unknown. Because past the fog—maybe even before we get out of it—there is something for us to learn, a way for us to grow, and a new thing that will shape our lives like nothing else could if we do not go into the unknown.

Just because we press forward does not mean we forget what we've experienced. It is because of who we've been and what we've experienced that we're prepared to move forward in confidence. Our lives cannot be bound by our current status. We can never forget the impact of family dinners, road trips with friends, late nights of conversation, and the moments shared with the best of people.

It is not the same for everyone. Many of us must stay where we are for a time because there is still something to be done. Do not mistake activity for progress; do not miss each moment's significance by dreaming only of the future.

Sometimes the journey is a new city and state, but sometimes it is a new commitment—a renewed sense of purpose within your present circumstances. No matter what kind of journey is before you, you must take it. You must go.

We must each take the journey because it is how God shapes us into who we're designed to be. We do not become someone we're not, but we become more deeply who we are. God's provision becomes evident in the variables of change, enduring conflict, and relationships that craft our lives.

The more variables you embrace, the greater beauty you'll

discover. This variable life requires your curiosity and your courage.

You must go.

The Move

Kati and I prepared and then made the move, because we knew those things rang true during our time in Oregon. And we expected it to become true in a new city, on a new coast.

We were headed for South Carolina, because we had an opportunity and a promise. The opportunity was a test of the lessons we had only begun to learn, to prove our willingness to depart the comfortable status quo and begin again in our unmistakable next stage. Our careers, relationships, and perspectives would evolve; they would have to if we were to adapt and grow. The promise was more than a new start, new friends, and a new home. It was God saying he'd go with us, into the unknown, into a new chapter within our story.

So we went.

Notes

1   Descartes, René, Valentine Rodger Miller, and Reese P. Miller. *Principles of Philosophy*. (Dordrecht, Holland: Reidel, 1983).

2   Andy Andrews, "3 Reasons Why You Should Take More Risks," April 25, 2012, http://www.andyandrews.com/3-reasons-why-you-should-take-more-risks/

3   1 Corinthians 16:13-14 (NIV)

4   Anaïs Nin, *D. H. Lawrence: An Unprofessional Study* (Chicago, IL: Swallow Press, 1964), 20.

5   Frank O'Hara, "In Memory of My Feelings," *The Collected Poems of Frank O'Hara*, edited by Donald Allen, University of California Press, 1956, p. 256.

6   Ta-Nehisi Coates, *Between the World and Me* (New York: Spiegel & Grau, 2015).

7   Mary Oliver, "Wild Geese," *Dream Work*, Atlantic Monthly Press, New York, NY, 1986.

8   Psalm 66:5 (NIV)

9   Psalm 66:12 (NIV)

10 Psalm 65:11 (NIV)

11 Psalm 66:16 (NIV)

12 Lamentations 3:19-33 (NLT)

13 Matthew 23:12, James 4:6

14 Anne Lamott, *Traveling Mercies: Some Thoughts on Faith* (New York: Pantheon Books, 1999), 143.

15 Ben Arment, *Dream Year: Make the Leap From a Job You Hate to a Life You Love* (New York: Portfolio/Penguin, 2014), 9.

16 Adam Piore, "What Technology Can't Change About Happiness," *Nautilus*, September 17, 2015, http://nautil.us/issue/28/2050/what-technology-cant-change-about-happiness

17 Bob Goff, *Love Does: Discover a Secretly Incredible Life in an Ordinary World* (Nashville, TN: Thomas Nelson, 2012), 118.

18 Susan Cain, *Quiet: The Power of Introverts in a World That Can't Stop Talking* (New York: Broadway Paperbacks, 2012), 4.

19 Brené Brown, *Daring Greatly: How the Courage to Be Vulnerable Transforms the Way We Live, Love, Parent, and Lead* (New York: Gotham Books, 2012), 8.

20 Sarah Bessey, *Jesus Feminist: An Invitation to Revisit the Bible's View of Women* (New York: Howard Books, 2013), 4.

21 Psalm 23:4 (NIV)

22 Psalm 23:5 (NIV)

23   Psalm 23:6 (NIV)

24   Psalm 23:6 (NIV)

25   Maya Angelou, *Letter to My Daughter* (New York: Random House, 2009).

26   Exodus 20:16 (NIV)

27   Attributed to Ernest Hemingway: "Develop a built-in bullshit detector." *The Gigantic Book of Teachers' Wisdom*, edited by Erin Gruwell (New York: Skyhorse Publishing, 2007), 147.

28   Rachel Held Evans, *A Year of Biblical Womanhood: How a Liberated Woman Found Herself Sitting on Her Roof, Covering Her Head, and Calling Her Husband "Master"* (Nashville: Thomas Nelson, 2012), 114.

29   Luke 19:1-10, Mark 9:35

30   Antonio Machado, "Proverbs and Folksongs," *Campos de Castilla.*, translated by Mary G. Berg and Dennis Maloney, White Pine Press, Buffalo, NY, 2005 , p. 239.

31   Matthew 5:48, 1 Peter 1:15-16 (NIV)

32   2 Timothy 4:7 (NIV)

33   Shauna Niequist, *Bread & Wine: A Love Letter to Life Around the Table* (Grand Rapids, MI: Zondervan, 2013).

34   Rob Bell interviewed by Ktizo Magazine. "The Way We Change is to Experience a Disruption. Interview with Rob Bell," Ross Gale, June 7, 2013, http://rcgale.com/2013/06/07/rob-bell-interview-art/

35   Attributed to Dr. Paul Tournier, https://www.goodreads.com/quotes/101973-nothing- makes-us-so-lonely-as-our-secrets

36   Genesis 2:21-22 37

37   Genesis 2:23

38   Danny Silk, *Keep Your Love On: Connection, Communication, and Boundaries* (Redding, CA: Red Arrow Media, 2013), 104.

39   John Muir, "Mt. Shasta," *Picturesque California: The Rocky Mountains and the Pacific Slope*, 1888, 165.

40   Edward Abbey, *Desert Solitaire: A Season in the Wilderness* (New York: Touchstone, Simon & Schuster, 1968), 169.

41   Susan Cain, "The Power of Introverts," TED2012, 28 February 2012, Long Beach, CA. Keynote speech.

42   Genesis 7:1-3, 1 Samuel 15:2-3, John 6:54

43   Saint Augustine, *Confessions*, translated by Henry Chadwick (New York: Oxford University Press Inc., 1992), 3.

44   English or Swahili proverb, sometimes attributed to Franklin D. Roosevelt. Weird, right?

45   Steven Pressfield, *The Warrior Ethos* (New York: Black Irish Entertainment LLC, 2011), 83.

46   1 John 4:18 (NIV)

47   Danny Silk, *Keep Your Love On* (Redding, CA: Red Arrow Media, 2013), 111.

48   Cheryl Strayed, *Tiny Beautiful Things: Advice on Love and Life from Dear Sugar* (New York: Vintage Books/Random House, 2012), 248.

49   Preston Sprinkle, *Fight: A Christian Case for Nonviolence* (Colorado Springs, CO: David C Cook, 2013), 47.

50   Exodus 21:1-6, Deuteronomy 15:12-18 51

51   1 Corinthians 6:19-20 (NIV)

52   Genesis 2:7, 21-22

53   Hebrews 12:2 (NKJV)

54   Galatians 4:1-7

55   Globalrichlist.com will rock your world.

56   Luke 12:48

57   Luke 11:9-13

58   Attributed to Saint Augustine, from a sermon on love.

59   Bob Hamp. "6 Characteristics of Spiritual Leaders." Michael Hyatt, 13 March 2012, http://michaelhyatt.com/characteristics-of-spiritual-leaders.html

60   Madeleine L'Engle, *A Wrinkle In Time* (New York: Square Fish/Macmillan, 1962), 60.

61   Sarah Green Carmichael. "The Research Is Clear: Long Hours Backfire for People and for Companies." *Harvard Business Review*, 19 Aug. 2015, https://hbr.org/2015/08/the-research-is-clear-long-hours-backfire-for-people-and-for-companies

62   Derek Thompson, "A World Without Work." *The Atlantic*, July/August 2015 issue, http://www.theatlantic.com/magazine/archive/2015/07/world-without-work/395294/

63   Ecclesiastes 1:1, 1:12 (NIV)

64   1 Kings 10:23-29, 1 Kings 11:1-6

65   Ecclesiastes 4:7-12 (NIV)

66   Best book I've read on the theology of work and rest: John Mark Comer, *Garden City: Work, Rest, and the Art of Being Human* (Grand Rapids, MI: Zondervan, 2015), 104.

67   Comer, *Garden City*, 120.

68   Brené Brown, *I Thought It Was Just Me (but it isn't): Making the Journey from "What Will People Think?" to "I Am Enough"* (New York: Avery/Penguin Random House, 2007).

69   1 John 2:9-10 (NIV)

70   John 16:24, Nehemiah 8:10, Romans 15:13

71   Matthew 22:36-40

72   1 John 3:1, 1 John 4:19-21

73   Proverbs 17:17 (NIV)

74   C. S. Lewis, *The Four Loves* (Orlando, FL: Harcourt, Inc., 1960), 57.

75   C. S. Lewis, *The Four Loves*, 89.

76   Isaiah 55:8-9 (NIV)

77   Philippians 1:3-7 (NIV)

78   Jim Collins, "Great by Choice." *Global Leadership Summit*. 10 Aug. 2012. Barrington, IL. Keynote speech.

79   Attributed to Malcolm S. Forbes.

80   Abraham Joshua Heschel, *The Sabbath: Its Meaning for Modern Man* (New York: Farrar, Straus, and Giroux, 1951).

81   John 10:1-10

82   John 10:10 (NKJV)

83   John 14:16-27

84   Austin Kleon, *Steal Like an Artist: 10 Things Nobody Told You About Being Creative* (New York: Workman Publishing Company, Inc., 2012), 94.

85   Attributed to Jimmy Dean, as well as Dolly Parton, Bertha Calloway, Thomas Monson, Cora Hatch, and Howard Agnew Johnston. Can someone get to the bottom of this?

86   Anaïs Nin, *The Diary of Anaïs Nin, Vol. 5: 1947-1955* (New York: Harcourt Brace Jovanovich, 1974).

87   Ben Arment, *Dream Year: Make the Leap From a Job You Hate to a Life You Love* (New York: Portfolio/Penguin, 2014), 24.

88   Steve Jobs, *Stanford University Commencement*, 12 June 2005, Stanford, CA. Keynote speech.

89   2 Timothy 2:13 (NIV)

90   Danny Silk, *Keep Your Love On: Connection, Communication, and Boundaries* (Redding, CA: Red Arrow Media, 2013), 99.

91   Philippians 4:7

92   Malcolm Gladwell, interviewed by Paul Holdengräber. *LIVE from the New York Public Library*, 1 April 2014, https://www.nypl.org/events/programs/2014/04/01/malcolm-gladwell-paul-holden-graber-0

93   Madeleine L'Engle, *A Wrinkle In Time* (New York: Square Fish/Macmillan, 1962), 25.

94   Rob Bell, *Velvet Elvis: Repainting the Christian Faith* (Grand Rapids, MI: Zondervan, 2005).

95   Shauna Niequist, *Bread & Wine: A Love Letter to Life Around the Table* (Grand Rapids, MI: Zondervan, 2013).

96   Chuck Klosterman, *Killing Yourself to Live: 85% of a True Story* (New York: Scribner, 2005), 217.

97   Genesis 2:4-25

98   Ephesians 5:21-33

99   Tim Keller with Kathy Keller, *The Meaning of Marriage: Facing the Complexities of Commitment with the Wisdom of God* (New York: Dutton/Penguin Group, 2011), 203.

100   Sarah Bessey, *Jesus Feminist: An Invitation to Revisit the Bible's View of Women* (New York: Howard Books, 2013), 83.

101   Kahlil Gibran, *The Prophet* (New York: Alfred A. Knopf, 1923).

102   Acts 9:1-9

103   Acts 9:10-19

104   2 Corinthians 12:7 (NIV)

105   2 Corinthians 12:8-9 (NIV) 106

106   2 Corinthians 12:10 (NIV)

107   G. K. Chesterton, *The Spice of Life: and other essays* (Philadelphia, PA: Dufour Editions, 1966).

108   Søren Kierkegaard, *Papers and Journals: A Selection*, translated by Alastair Hannay (New York: Penguin Group: 1996), 295.

109   Sherry Turkle, "Stop Googling. Let's Talk." *The New York Times*. 26 Sept. 2015, http://www.nytimes.com/2015/09/27/opinion/sunday/stop-googling-lets-talk.html

110   Italo Calvino, *Difficult Loves*, translated by William Weaver, Archibald Colquhoun, and Peggy Wright (Orlando, FL: Harcourt Brace & Company, 1984), 225.

111   Donald Miller, *Scary Close: Dropping the Act and Finding True Intimacy* (Nashville, TN: Nelson Books/Thomas Nelson: 2014), 171.

112   Mary Oliver. "Sometimes." *Red Bird*. (Boston, MA: Beacon Press, 2008), 37.

113   Filmmaker Salomon Ligthelm, "The Great Abyss with Salomon Ligthelm," *YouTube*, uploaded by The Music Bed, 2 April 2014, https://youtu.be/i8r3o3zuPbs

114   2 Corinthians 4:8-12 (NIV)

115   Walter Brueggemann. "A Conversation with Walter Brueggemann," Interview by Bradford Winters. *Image Journal*, Issue 55, http://imagejournal.org/article/conversation-walter-brueggemann/

116   *The Declaration of Independence*. United States of America, 4 July 1776.

117   Daniel 3:1-30, Philippians 3:20

118   Isaiah 1:11-20, Acts 10:34-48, Galatians 3:28

119   Anne Lamott, *Help, Thanks, Wow: The Three Essential Prayers* (New York: Riverhead Books/ Penguin Group, 2012).

120   2 Corinthians 1:3-4 (NIV)

121   Mark Batterson, *Wild Goose Chase: Reclaim the Adventure of Pursuing God* (Colorado Springs, CO: Multnomah Books/Random House, 2008), 50.

122   Matthew 5:2-12, Matthew 13:44-45, Luke 15:1-32

123   1 Peter 2:11-12 (NLT)

124   Jeremiah 29:1-23, Daniel 1:1-3:30

125   1 Peter 2:11 (NLT), Philippians 3:20 (NIV)

126   Attributed to Oliver Wendell Holmes, Sr.

127   N. T. Wright's *Surprised By Hope* and John Mark Comer's *Garden City* are superb. C. S. Lewis' *The Great Divorce* will spark your imagination.

128   Luke 10:9, Matthew 10:7-8, Luke 14:7-24

129   Matthew 6:9-10, Luke 12:31-32, John 3:3, Isaiah 9:6-7

130   Watchman Nee, *A Table in the Wilderness* (Fort Washington, PA: CLC Publications, 1957), May 15 entry.

131   Revelation 21:1-5

132   Colossians 1:19-20

133   2 Corinthians 5:1-21

134   Antoine de Saint-Exupéry, *The Little Prince*, translated by Richard Howard (Orlando, FL: Harcourt, Inc., 1943), 65.

135   Bertrand Piccard. "Public Speaking in brief." BertrandPiccard.com. http://bertrandpiccard.com/ publicspeaking-in-brief

136   Anne Lamott, Help, Thanks, *Wow: The Three Essential Prayers* (New York: Riverhead Books/ Penguin Group, 2012).

137   John 10:10, Luke 4:18

138   Attributed to Wendell Berry, http://www.goodreads.com/quotes/102492-if-you-don-t-know-where-you-re-from-you-ll-have-a

139   2 Corinthians 4:15-18 (NIV)

140   Rachel Held Evans, Searching for *Sunday: Loving, Leaving, and Finding the Church* (Nashville, TN: Nelson Books/Thomas Nelson, 2015), 225.

141   Attributed to W. H. Auden.

142   Thornton Wilder, *Our Town: A Play in Three Acts* (New York: Coward-McCann, Inc. with Samuel French, Inc., 1938), 68.

143   Elie Wiesel, *The Gates of the Forest* (Austin, TX: Holt, Rinehart, and Winston, 1966).

Thanks

To all the people in these stories, thank you for helping me see what humanity is capable of: the good and the bad and the redeemable. You prove life is full of variables, that it can look all sorts of ways, and that is okay.

Thanks to every editor who's read my work, taken a chance on me, and said yes. Especially the ones who said yes again and again.

Thanks to my editor Chantel Hamilton, who is sharp as she is kind. This manuscript needed you, and I'm grateful for your editorial expertise and wisdom that refined its heart and smoothed its rough edges. If only more of us lived like you edit: drawing out the purpose and personality of every story. Thanks also to Katie O'Hara for helping with finishing touches.

Thanks to my designer, Ben Coleman, who's done far more than arrange visuals and text. You've taught me how to show up to my own curiosity, relationships, and life. The diamonds shine on, my friend.

Mom and Dad, thank you for providing the resources, opportunities, and encouragement to keep growing. Mom, you've always called me a writer; I just needed time to see it for myself. Dad, you've always talked about working hard and doing right by others; you lived it out, too. Both of you make me stronger.

Laura and Lee, we've grown up together, fought each other, and loved each other like only siblings can. You've taught me how to live in proximity with family and choose love, to extend and receive grace. I'll never forget those family road trips. Thanks for sharing your journey with each other and with me.

Laura, Mark, and Nicole, you have taught me how to be in a new family, and it is good. Thank you for welcoming me and being a foundation Kati and I treasure. I still remember that artichoke dinner.

Kati, thank you for letting this book and these ideas invade our schedule, energy, and attention. But even more, thank you for building this togetherness we share, for taking the leaps with me when it's easier to stay comfortable, and for adapting along the way. We're still on that scavenger hunt. Love is always a risk, and you are worth it.

God, I sense I'm only just beginning to know you, the real you, and you keep showing up in the most curious ways. Thank you for the mystery and the gift we call life.

To my community, thank you for the years I've spent with each of you in different churches, cities, and stages of life. You have shown me grace and truth across the table, on the trail, around the living room, through phone calls and video chats, during carpools and airport pickups, and in a million other ways. I'm lucky to have you. Most grateful thanks to Brian, Danielle, Seth, Shea, Nate, Robyn, David, and Karli.

To the fine folks who read early drafts of this manuscript and told me it wasn't complete garbage, thank you: Bradley Miller, Seth Ray, Nate Ray, and Nick Charalambous.

To Stephanie Long, thank you for collaborating on projects for this book, your editorial assistance, and the support of a fellow introvert writer. You are teaching us all through your vulnerability and your pursuit of what's true.

To every supporter on Kickstarter, thank you a thousand times over. You believed in this book enough to get it off the ground and into the hands of more people.

Diamond Level Supporters
Seth and Shea Ray
Jim and Jill Weirick
In honor of John and Harriette Weirick

Platinum Level Supporters
Susy and Jon Ramthun
Brian and Danielle Kalwat

Gold Level Supporters
Roberta Hodgen
David and Karli Stevens
Brenda and Alex de Hoyos
Nate and Robyn Ray
Jason and Christine Agee
Tim and Mandee Prince
Chris and Missy Masterjohn
Edolyne and Stephanie Long
Tobias Maier
Sabine and Joerg Maier
Garth West
Mark and Laura Stanislawski
Steve Weirick
Ricky and Krista Ortiz
Bradley Miller
Daniel and Kelsey McLaughlin
Matt and Carrie Ystad
Sang You

Silver Level Supporters
Christian, Justine, and Ezra Schaefer
Judy Hughes

Bob Smith
Bruce Stevens
Tyler Krumholz
Joel Morgan
Brennan Ullom
Ricky Nelson
Kim Bolton
Stephen Ramthun
Jacqui Griggs
Leo Endel
Matt and Diana Sanders

Bronze Level Supporters
Rachel Dawson
Darious Smith
Robert "The Bob-O" Curry
Rich and Laurie Hefty
Kyle Vines
Josh Downey
Jenna Olson
Bradley and Lu Anne Gafford
Tanner Olson
Allison Rickard
Kevin Caldwell
James and Holly Baxley
Tim McLaughlin
Jesse and Jessica Bittmann
Tim and Rachel Nafziger
Ryan Weirick
Allen Cothran
Bob and Marilyn Kalwat
Nick and Katie Ristow
Christopher Molenaar
Josh Williams

Andrew and Ariel Schibilla
Branden Harvey
Sean Sullivan
Eric Philbert
Lauren Carawan
Michael Gay
Marc McComas
Emily Becker
Andrew Gafford
John Pinkerton
Brian and Kristie Jones
Matthew Bradford
Dylan and Bridget Gregory

To you, reading this book, thank you for venturing with me through these pages and stories. I'd love to hear how you're navigating your own variable life. Say hello at john@johnweirick.com.

About the Author

John Weirick is a writer on faith, culture, and relationships. His work has been featured on *The Huffington Post*, *RELEVANT Magazine*, and dozens of online publications with millions of readers. John lives in Greenville, South Carolina and online at johnweirick.com.

Follow him on:
Facebook.com/johnweirick
Twitter (@johnweirick)
Instagram (@johnweirick)

Share quotes with #TheVariableLife.

Visit thevariablelife.com for more.

Made in the USA
Charleston, SC
15 February 2017